JOHN BRADSHAW

P9-CRZ-681

CONFIDENCE in CHAOS

REVIEW AND HERALD® PUBLISHING ASSOCIATION
Since 1861 | www.reviewandherald.com

Published by Review and Herald® Publishing Association, Hagerstown, MD 21741-1119

The Review and Herald® Publishing Association publishes biblically based materials for spiritual, physical, and mental growth and Christian discipleship.

Review and Herald® titles may be purchased in bulk for educational, business, fund-raising, or sales promotional use. For information, e-mail SpecialMarkets@reviewandherald.com.

Unless otherwise noted, Bible texts in this book are from the New King James Version. Copyright © 1979, 1980, 1982 by Thomas Nelson, Inc. Used by permission. All rights reserved.

This book was
Edited by Gerald Wheeler
Copyedited by Megan Mason
Interior Design by Derek Knecht/Review and Herald® Design Center
Cover Design by Bryan Gray/Review and Herald® Design Center
Typeset: Minion Pro 10/12

PRINTED IN U.S.A.

18 17 16 15 14   5 4 3 2

Library of Congress Control Number: 2013944916

ISBN 978-0-8280-2757-1

CONFIDENCE in CHAOS

Contents

CHAPTER 1

A World in Crisis

Have you heard about the bombing?"
My eyes widened with surprise and concern. Soon I'd be feeling sadness and anger. "The bombing? What bombing? I haven't heard a thing." My pulse quickened.

It was early morning; I had gone for breakfast in a European hotel. I had just conducted an evangelistic series in the city of Prague in the Czech Republic, and several of us were now on a tour of various Reformation sites. The cold of winter had begun giving way to the gentle warmth of spring, and the day stretching before us promised adventure and discovery. Mayhem was the last thing on my mind.

"There's been a bombing at the Boston Marathon," Ed explained. "Two bombs."

The Boston Marathon! I thought to myself. There's no way this could be anything other than a total disaster. Quickly I fired off the questions you would expect: How many casualties? Has anyone claimed responsibility? Was it an act of terrorism? Are you sure it was bombs? What's going on?

In time details of the tragedy emerged. Remarkably, the authorities released photos of the suspected bombers just days after the atrocity that killed three people and injured more than 260. Two young men, one in a white baseball cap turned backward, the other wearing a black baseball cap, both of them carrying backpacks, had been caught on camera as they sauntered through the unsuspecting crowd on a perfectly fine spring day. A day that—senselessly— turned out to be thoroughly imperfect.

The Boston bombings captured the attention of the

nation as television news channels provided round-the-clock coverage of the unfolding drama. Americans were glued to their televisions and computer screens as one of the nation's major cities experienced a tumultuous four days of fear and apprehension.

Following the horror of September 11, 2001, the specter of terrorism on American soil has occupied a prominent place in the national psyche. Newscasters and others repeatedly asked, "Who would do such a thing? Will the bombers strike again? Are they part of a larger organization?" And most of all: "Was this the work of terrorists?"

The United States—especially the city of Boston—was anxious.

Two days after the Boston Marathon bombings, a massive explosion occurred at a fertilizer company in the small town of West, Texas, located along Interstate 35 about an hour south of Fort Worth. The blast killed 15, injured more than 160, and destroyed more than 150 buildings. Video footage of the massive fireball left many people incredulous that the death toll wasn't far higher. At the time the devastating explosion occurred, emergency services were already at the plant fighting a fire.

The day after the Boston bombings and the one before the deadly explosion at the fertilizer company 20 minutes north of Waco, Texas, a letter at a government mail facility in Washington, D.C., tested positive for ricin, a deadly substance derived from castor beans. The letter was addressed to a senator from the state of Mississippi. The next day a letter to President Barack Obama also had traces of ricin, as did a third letter received by a Mississippi judge.

Terrorism targeting innocent people at an iconic sporting event; an enormous explosion that looked like something out of a Hollywood action movie; and letters tainted with a deadly toxin sent to the president of the United States? All within three days? It felt very much like America was under siege. The nation seemed to be going through a serious crisis.

Perhaps we could regard three terrible events in three days as a coincidence. And perhaps *crisis* is a relative term. Maybe it is that even stable, secure nations experience horrifying attacks on innocent civilians, the tragic destruction of lives and property, and assassination attempts on its president as a matter of course.

But then again, perhaps not.

The Bible predicted that "in the last days perilous times will come," a period when people will be "unholy," "unloving," "brutal," and "despisers of good" (2 Timothy 3:1-4). Even a cursory look around the world gives ample evidence that we've reached the condition that Paul wrote to Timothy about. And we have a whole lot more than three unrelated events[1] by which to gauge that we're living in an era of real crisis.

Think about just some of what we've been experiencing that suggests that the time in which we live is like no other.

On September 11, 2001, aircraft filled with fuel and passengers slammed into the World Trade Center in New York City, the Pentagon in Washington, D.C., and the ground near Shanksville, Pennsylvania. In all, thousands died, and life would never again be the same for large sections of the world's population, with increased security measures encroaching into nearly every area of life.

Before long it became known that Middle Eastern terrorism groups had committed the September 11 attacks. And as horrifying as they were, Middle Eastern terrorism was something with which the world was already sadly familiar. The World Trade Center had already endured an attack in 1993. Middle Eastern terrorists detonated a truck bomb in an attempt to cause the north tower of the World Trade Center to fall onto the south tower, destroying both buildings and causing massive loss of life. Although that catastrophe never materialized, six people perished and more than 1,000 suffered injuries. Six men were convicted in relation to the bombing.

As conflicting as it is to admit, terrorism has become

part of the fabric of our lives. Not that the average person living in the heartland has to dodge terrorists as they go about their daily lives. But whether through laws passed, security measures put in place, or simply by the lack of surprise expressed when terrorists strike, it is clear that terrorism is now a fact of life.

But what was so disturbing about the Boston Marathon bombings wasn't simply that the attacks took place. What many people found truly shocking was the manner in which they occurred.

Two young, likable men mingled with the buoyant crowd on a beautiful spring morning and casually left their homemade explosive devices—made from pressure cookers!—in position to kill and maim. They had not trained in a terror camp in Afghanistan, as the World Trade Center bombers had. Instead, they had learned how to build bombs from an Internet Web site.

And they were *young* men. One was 26, and the other just 19 years old. At a time when most men their age would be pursuing a career or hanging out with friends, the two bombers were planning a killing spree that they intended would end as many lives as possible.

Terrorism is no longer the domain of the advanced bombmaking expert, nor does it require aircraft or high-caliber weapons. The Boston bombings added a destabilizing element not seen before in terroristic activity: the alleged perpetrators allegedly crafted their implements of death barely 30 miles from where the carnage occurred. They were home-grown, backyard terrorists. The terrorists next door. Gone are the days when terrorism was the domain of unfamiliar-looking foreigners who slipped illegally into a country or assumed false identities or lived double lives. One of the two young men was studying at a respected college and had expressed a desire to be a dentist.

If all this doesn't represent a crisis, I don't know what does.

And that raises an interesting point about crises. A crisis is definitely one when it affects *you*. When it touches someone else in a part of the country or of the world that you're totally unfamiliar with, it's less of a crisis and more of a crying shame. "What a shame about those attacks! That's just too bad. Think of it—here, in this country . . . Well, must take the dog for a walk."

Genocide in Rwanda is a tragedy of immense proportions, but it's easy to see it as somebody else's problem when you're removed from it by thousands of miles. A tornado tearing through someone else's town is disastrous. But when it smashes through *your* town—and it's *you* who's sifting through the ruins of your home picking baby photos out of the mud, and you don't have a place to sleep or clean water to drink—then it's a *crisis*.

On many levels we've reached a crisis point as a planet. The reason this is important on a spiritual level is that in Matthew 24 Jesus went to great lengths to point out the observable signs that would portend the end of the world and His return to earth.

And what Jesus said then indicates strongly that we're now living in the time to which He referred.

Having spoken of signs in the religious world, of international conflicts, natural disasters and disease, He announced His second coming by saying, "So you also, when you see all these things, know that it is near—at the doors!" (Matthew 24:33). It certainly isn't alarmist to believe we're living in the crisis that precedes the return of Jesus. And while there's no question things are going to get worse before they get better, wisdom suggests that people should read such signs for what they are: indicators that time is short for Planet Earth, and—not knowing just how brief that might be—that now is when we should be certain our lives are in the hands of the God of heaven. Or, as Peter wrote: "Be even more diligent to make your call and election sure" (2 Peter 1:10).

I'm as aware as anyone that through the years people seeking to impress upon others the shortness of time have written and said a lot of embarrassing things. One of the first books I read on the subject of Bible prophecy seemed to imply that Jesus' return could take place in 1988. One author—who first suggested that Christ might appear in 1994—later predicted the rapture would take place on May 21, 2011, and that the world would come to an end five months later.

When still a brand-new Christian, I read about a Korean group predicting the coming of Jesus on a specific day. We kidded about it as we left work that day before the forecast apocalypse, "See you tomorrow—maybe!" But none of us thought for a moment the world was going to end that night. And deep down I felt pity, knowing that somewhere were those who believed strongly enough in the return of Jesus taking place on the specified date that they were willing to donate their money and sacrifice their reputation. And they were going to be very disappointed.

Since then—more than 20 years ago—people who have attached dates to the prophecies of the Bible have come and gone. Unsurprisingly, every one of them has been dead wrong.

But failed predictions are not merely a recent phenomenon. While you might not call their view a "prediction" as such, even the disciples of Jesus had it wrong about the coming of the Messiah. Very, very wrong.

On the very day Jesus ascended to heaven, the disciples asked Him, "'Lord, will You at this time restore the kingdom to Israel?' And He said to them, 'It is not for you to know times or seasons which the Father has put in His own authority. But you shall receive power when the Holy Spirit has come upon you; and you shall be witnesses to Me in Jerusalem, and in all Judea and Samaria, and to the end of the earth'" (Acts 1:6-8).

In spite of having spent more than three years with Jesus;

in spite of having cast out demons and healed the sick in Jesus' name; in spite of having witnessed miracles—multitudes fed, the dead raised, the sick healed, a storm calmed—in spite of having been instructed by the best Bible Teacher who had ever lived, the disciples were still able to be incredibly wrong about a fundamental tenet of Scripture. Even they were confused about the return of Jesus!

During His ministry they had argued about who among them should be greatest, to the extent that two of the disciples petitioned that He reserve for them the preeminent place in what they believed to be His soon-established kingdom.

"Then James and John, the sons of Zebedee, came to Him, saying, 'Teacher, we want You to do for us whatever we ask.' And He said to them, 'What do you want Me to do for you?' They said to Him, 'Grant us that we may sit, one on Your right hand and the other on Your left, in Your glory'" (Mark 10:35-37).

And they did this in spite of Jesus having told them numerous times that He was going to be crucified (see Matthew 17:22; Mark 8:31; 10:33, 34; Matthew 26:2, etc.)! It seems the modern predilection for false theories about Christ's return has roots that run deep.

Baptist preacher William Miller led a group of Christian believers—primarily in the American northeast—who were convinced that Jesus was going to return in the year 1843. Many of them quit their jobs, walked off their land, and gave away their possessions in the belief that they no longer needed them. When the 1843 prediction failed, they suggested their mathematical calculation of certain prophetic periods had been off by one year. Jesus would come in 1844. And, of course, He did not.

But then again, what's a person to do? Jesus spoke so much about His second advent that it would be only natural for people to talk about it, pray about it, look forward to it—and wonder when it might be. Even Eve—the second person created—in a way predicted the coming of the Messiah. The original Hebrew of Genesis 4:1 records her as having said after the birth of her firstborn son, "I have gotten a man, the Lord." Eve had never forgotten the promise God made to her and Adam in Genesis 3:15, when He said, "And I will put enmity between you and the woman, and between your seed and her Seed; He shall bruise your head, and you shall bruise His heel."

Understandably, at the birth of her first son Eve thought the promised Seed had arrived, failing to understand that the Messiah would not enter the world until several millennia had passed. In her day it was absolutely impossible to gauge when the Messiah might come. But that's not the case today.

While history reveals the folly of setting dates for the coming of Jesus, God has told us clearly that we could know when it would grow near. And that's where we are today. Near.

And how can we be so sure? One reason is that the world is in crisis. Now, having said that, *crisis* is a highly subjective term. Whether or not you perceive something as a crisis depends on several factors, including your vantage point.

To those living during World War II and directly affected by its horrors, the period from 1939 to 1945 was undoubtedly a crisis. If you found yourself in London during the Blitz in 1940 and 1941, when the German Luftwaffe rained bombs down on it and other British cities—killing more than 40,000 people and destroying more than 1 million homes in London alone—you'd no doubt label the experience a crisis. Those trapped in the German city of Dresden in the closing months of World War II, when the British and American air forces barraged the city with bombs and incendiary devices—burning 15 square miles of the city and wiping out around 25,000 people—would have called the event a crisis. We could say the same for those in concentration camps. If Auschwitz-Birkenau wasn't a crisis of the worst kind, then nothing can be called a crisis.

But did World War II—or World War I, or Vietnam, or the stock market crash of 1929, or the San Francisco earthquake, or any other similar event—indicate that the return of Jesus was imminent?

Jesus gave us signs to read. Verifiable, concrete signs. Empirical evidence. He said, "Look for this, you'll be able to see that, and you'll notice something else." This isn't like reading tea leaves.

Some years ago the program director at the radio station where I worked told me he had arranged for a special guest to join me on air. One of the country's best-known psychics had agreed to spend an hour or two taking calls from listeners. Even though my program was predominantly a music program, the psychic was such a draw and so well known that interrupting the regular format of the program wasn't going to be a problem. And sure enough, more than 30 minutes before the program even began, all of the studio's many phone lines were busy.

Partway through the program, during a commercial break, the psychic started asking me questions. "I'm seeing some people behind you," she told me in a voice that wouldn't have been out of place as the narrator of a creepy documentary.

My eyebrows raised. "Oh?"

"Yes, four people. Four." She paused.

"H'mmm," I shrugged. "Who could that be?"

Even though I had no knowledge of what the Bible said on the subject, I'd never been a believer in ghosts. Yet she was seeing four people standing behind me?

"They're men. Four men. Four men who are important to you."

She waited for me to respond before she said, "Are there four men that are important to you?"

"Well, I do have four brothers," I offered.

After allowing herself a self-satisfied smile, she said, "Yes, that's who it would have been," before moving on to take the next caller I welcomed to the program.

If it hadn't been for my four brothers, without question

I'd have been able to find four other men important to me. My father, my rugby coach, an uncle, and my boss. What she was doing was simply setting me up to supply her information that she could claim had come to her supernaturally.

Being a psychic can be risky, however. In fact, American celebrity Sylvia Browne found herself under fire in 2013 after the discovery of three young women who had been missing for 10 years. In 2004 on national television she had told the mother of one of the girls that her daughter was dead. One subsequent investigation concluded that rather than the 87 to 90 percent success rate Ms. Browne claimed for her predictions, her success rate was a rather more modest 0 percent.

It's true that some—maybe many—predictions aren't worth the paper they're printed on, but in looking at the world around us and analyzing what we see in relation to the prophecies of the Bible, we're not *predicting* anything. The One who made the predictions was *Jesus*. All we need to do is open our eyes—and our hearts—to see that what He foretold has long begun to come to pass.

But while today few within mainstream Christianity are prepared to set specific dates for the second coming of Jesus, what is far more common is a "soft" form. You might have heard it yourself: "Now, I'm not claiming that this means Jesus is really going to return in the next 10 years, but what I'm saying is that it *could* mean that. It certainly looks interesting!"

Such speculation doesn't help anyone, and we should avoid it like the plague. We just don't know exactly when Jesus will come back. God hasn't given that information. The Bible simply doesn't say. But we can know when Jesus' return will be *near*.

Important? You better believe it. It's true that some have a type of "Matthew 24 fatigue," a jadedness, perhaps even a cynicism, toward the study of eschatology and the seeming hype that accompanies prognostications about the "end-times." And that may be because of the speculative or sensationalistic way some have handled the topic.

Instead of trying to figure how many days it is until Jesus returns; instead of worrying out loud in front of our children about how terrible the last days are going to be; instead of seeing every earthquake as a harbinger of the mark of the beast, we should see the signs of the times as what they really are. Signs. Of the days in which we live. And the period in which we live is close to the return of Jesus.

My wife and I have driven across the United States on numerous occasions, most often on Interstate 40. Stretching all the way from North Carolina in the east of the continent to California in the west, I-40 is 2,555 miles long, and we've traveled all but 200 miles of it several times in both directions. When you're heading out of the Mojave Desert with several days on the road ahead of you, it isn't very important to know just how many miles it is to where you're going. No doubt you would have a rough idea, and you recognize that if you make so much progress each day you will get to where you're going about the right time.

But what is vital is to be sure which road you're on. If you're coming into Barstow and you're headed for North Carolina, what's most important isn't how far you have to travel. Even though a sign on I-40 in Barstow announces, "Wilmington, N.C., 2,554 miles," your primary concern is making sure you don't take a wrong turn. Should you turn on to I-15 you will have wasted time and be headed in the wrong direction. What you want is I-40. So how can you know one road from the other?

Because we did the majority of our cross-country driving in the days before GPS became ubiquitous, we had to rely on old-fashioned tools such as maps. Maps and *signs*. If we're heading to North Carolina, we're making sure we're on Interstate 40; and the way you know that for sure is by looking for the blue-and-red shield-shaped sign with "40" emblazoned on it.

Even after driving for a day or two, the distance left to travel isn't a driver's primary concern. That is, you know you have two or three days of travel left. But as long as every now and then the signs saying "40" come into view, you realize that you are on the right road.

In fact, unless your destination is a major city, it isn't usually until you get close to it that signs appear stating how many miles you have left. And it's a lot like that with the signs of Jesus' return. An earthquake or a war doesn't mean anyone should rush to look at the eastern sky to see if Jesus is on His way (see Matthew 24:30). But while those things don't necessarily indicate His return is imminent, they do suggest that we can have confidence in what Jesus said—particularly when the signs are occurring with frequency and fury.

The Bible has alerted us that we will be living in a time of real crisis before Jesus comes back. The prophet Daniel described it as being "a time of trouble, such as never was since there was a nation" (Daniel 12:1). Paul called earth's final days "perilous" (2 Timothy 3:1), and Jesus predicted that there would be a "great tribulation" (Matthew 24:21). As my children would say when they were very young and we were pulling out of our driveway with a long journey ahead of us, "Are we nearly there yet?"

In his recent book *Planet in Distress,* author Scott Christiansen wrote that the rapid decline of global systems— when compared with what the Bible says about earth's last days—indicate that we are indeed living in a time of crisis.

Carefully investigating the world's major "systems"— climate, food production, water, energy, and so on— Christiansen showed that Planet Earth is at a breaking point. And it seems that before long something's gotta give.

In 1927 the world had 2 billion people. Then, less than 100 years later, the planet had added more than 5 billion more. It is dramatic to see such a population explosion plotted on a graph.

True, nothing guarantees that population growth will

continue at such a breakneck pace. The United Nations Population Fund (UNPF) predicts the rate is about to start slowing as birthrates begin to decline. But even if—as the UNPF predicts—the world's population maxes out at a little more than 10 billion about 100 years from now, that may well place too great a strain on our planet's resources and its ability to recover from centuries of abuse at the hands of the human race.

The planet's soaring population requires an ever-increasing amount of food. Food production has become increasingly industrialized, to the extent that today the enormous amounts of energy, pesticides, and fertilizers used in it have worn out a dramatic amount of the planet's soil. Scott Christiansen writes that since 1945, approximately 45 percent of the earth's vegetated surface has been degraded.[2] Massive amounts of land are abandoned, often replaced through slash-and-burn deforestation.[3]

Various places around the globe are experiencing severe water shortages. A recent CNN report that I watched stated that "thousands" of rivers in China have dried up in recent years. Recently I saw firsthand how unbelievably polluted the air is in some parts of the world. While I had thought the air quality in Los Angeles was bad, I was shocked with what I encountered in India. The pollution was so bad—and so visible—that I asked my traveling companion if a fire was burning somewhere nearby. A couple days later I read in the *Times of India*—the world's largest-selling English-language daily newspaper—that air pollution is India's fifth-largest killer. Many claim China's air pollution is even worse, with media reports frequently commenting on the ecological disaster occurring in the world's most populous nation.

Now, maybe Planet Earth has some way it can recover from this. Perhaps climate change is reversible.[4] The Chinese might clean up their air. And the water table could recover. But it will be difficult. In August of 2012 the *Christian Science Monitor* reported that central Georgia has joined the states of Texas, Nebraska, and Kansas in experiencing serious groundwater depletion. That is, the amount of water underground is getting more scarce.[5]

More mundane ecological issues don't get as much recognition as climate change, but promise to do calamitous damage to the environment. National Geographic reported that data from the 2012-2013 winter season indicates that beekeepers lost almost 50 percent of their hives, with disease threatening the very existence of bees in North America and around the world. A beekeeper friend of mine told me himself that he fears his industry is on the brink of collapse. And as bad as that would be, worse would be the consequences to the planet if it didn't have enough bees to pollinate the world's plants—especially those upon which we depend for our survival.

Add to this the proliferation in natural disasters in recent years. Twelve disasters alone during 2011—including hurricanes, tornadoes, and floods—caused more than $1 billion worth of damage each, with the National Oceanic and Atmospheric Administration announcing that the year's weather was the most extreme on record.[6] If you were to think back on the worst natural disasters you can remember, you'd realize that they've all taken place in the past 10 years or so. And experts say they're getting worse.[7]

Much has been said about the health-care crisis in the United States. First Lady Michelle Obama adopted obesity as her cause of major concern, because of the fact that while millions of people struggle to find enough food to eat, and while a child dies every five seconds as a result of hunger-related causes, millions of Americans overeat.[8] Approximately 42 Americans die each day from AIDS, and one person every 11 seconds worldwide. Approximately 26 million Americans—more than 8 percent of the nation's population—suffer from diabetes, and another 79 million Americans are classified as prediabetic. About 27 million Americans have been diagnosed with heart disease, with approximately 615,000 of them dying from the condition each year.

And then we could add to that a whole host of diseases that have reared their ugly heads only in more recent times. SARS, Avian Flu, and some truly scary things, such as the antibiotic-resistant bugs that ABC News reported in March 2013,[9] show that the picture—and the outlook—isn't pretty.

So let's consider: terrorism, runaway population growth, soil degradation, water shortages, killer pollution, ecological chaos, natural disasters, health crises, disease. And we haven't talked about the economy or a host of other things—such as violence.

Someone with a gun fires randomly into a crowd at a New Orleans Mother's Day parade, wounding 19 people. A desperately unbalanced young man killed 26 people (including 20 first-grade children) at an elementary school in Connecticut in December 2012. But I'm going to go out on a limb here and suggest that you don't even remember that eight months earlier a gunman at a Christian college in Oakland, California, forced the students in a nursing class to line up against a wall, then shot and killed seven of them, and wounded three others. In 2007 a 23-year-old man shot and killed 32 students and faculty members at Virginia Tech in Blacksburg, Virginia.

And yes, there have been school shootings before those. Natural disasters before those. Public health issues before those. Ecological and environmental challenges before those. And terrorism before now. That's true. But it hasn't ever been like it is now. Ever.

If what we're living through is normal, then let's just roll over and go back to sleep. But it isn't possible to witness the world around us and begin to contemplate that this is anything approximating normal. The planet is in crisis.

So now what?

---

[1] In fact, the incidents are far from unrelated. Behind all sin

and suffering is Satan. Revelation 12:12 says he currently works with "great wrath, because he knows that he has a short time."

[2] Scott Christiansen, *Planet in Distress* (Hagerstown, Md.: Review and Herald Pub. Assn., 2012), p. 45.

[3] *Ibid.*

[4] And—some would say—perhaps it doesn't exist. But if you've been to places such as Glacier National Park and have seen where glaciers used to be and what they are like now, you'd have to admit that—climate change or not—*something* certainly is going on.

[5] Some say that there's only enough water left in the Ogallala Aquifer—the water table located beneath America's Great Plains—to last 25 more years. If that's not a crisis today, it's certainly going to be one tomorrow.

[6] http://washingtonpost.com/blogs/blogpost/post/was-2011-the-year-of-disasters/2011/12/08/gIQADnKzrO_blog.html.

[7] The headline in the Washington *Post* read, "Prepare Yourself, Natural Disasters Will Only Get Worse." http://articles.washingtonpost.com/2011-09-15/national/35274771_1_natural-disasters-hurricane-irene-earthquakes.

[8] Recognizing there is more than one cause for obesity.

[9] http://abcnews.go.com/Health/cre-tops-list-scary-superbugs/story?id=18666434#.UZazL7SyfzI.

CHAPTER 2

A Church in Crisis

In 2012 I was in Paris, France, to conduct a series of Bible lectures intended to provide impetus and inspiration for people to make a decision to accept Jesus as Lord and Savior. The meetings went wonderfully well and concluded with a major baptismal service in which scores of people in that secular city gave their lives to Jesus Christ.

During my time in Paris I visited Notre Dame Cathedral several times, mostly to use as a location for filming *It Is Written* television programs. And I had been to Notre Dame years before when in the city to see a rugby game: New Zealand versus France. When our bus arrived, it took us to Notre Dame early on a Saturday morning. But being hungry—and confident that I'd soon be back in Paris to see the fabled Cathedral—I opted to eat breakfast with a friend rather than tour the magnificent landmark. But now I was back, my "soon" being 22 years later!

Now I had time to see the cathedral itself. On this sunny spring day visitors from Russia packed Notre Dame. They had traveled to Paris especially to venerate the cathedral's most precious and most revered religious relic: the crown of thorns. The very crown of thorns Jesus had worn when He died on the cross.

In actual fact, even though it is called the crown of thorns, the prized relic had no thorns on it. They had long ago been separated from the crown itself, leaving only a circle of canes.

On the first Friday of every month the cathedral holds a special service to display the "crown." We were allowed to enter while it was under way, and I saw firsthand hundreds of dedicated worshippers come to the front of the church, and, one by one, stand before the object. All made the sign of the cross. Many bowed low to the ground, and a large number of the faithful kissed the floor in front of the "crown." All appeared deeply moved.

I, on the other hand, was aghast. The crown of thorns? That Jesus wore? For centuries churches have told their adherents that they possess this or that special relic that—when honored—might bring with it special blessing from God. Notre Dame Cathedral boasts that in addition to the crown Jesus wore on the cross, they also have in their possession a piece of the cross on which He died and one of the nails that held Him to the cross. I suspect that if you gathered all of the so-called pieces of Jesus' cross in one place, you would have enough wood to reconstruct Noah's ark, let alone the cross from Calvary.

As a child attending church at Eastertime, adults encouraged me to kiss "the wood of the cross on which our Savior died." They told me that a part of the cross we venerated had been made from wood that came from the very cross upon which Jesus was crucified. Our church—St. Paul's church—contained another relic, a fragment of bone from the apostle himself.

Whether people related things to me in good faith or not, I do not know. But they certainly were nothing more than stories designed to impress upon me the grandeur of my church and the authority it wielded.

When I asked an important-looking official at Notre Dame what the people were honoring, he explained in solemn tones that it was indeed the crown that had rested upon Jesus' brow during the final few hours of His earthly life.

In spite of our enlightenment, in spite of Google, in spite of advanced education and the cynical spirit of our age, plenty of Christians are still perfectly willing to accept such accounts unquestioningly. And plenty of church leaders are willing to relate them.

While in a foreign country, I flipped through the channels on the TV in my hotel room looking for news coverage of the Boston Marathon bombings. Finding a religious channel in English—featuring a sermon preached by an American preacher—I stopped to listen for a moment. I'll never forget what I saw and heard.

Speaking in one of those churches in which wealth and prosperity seem to be the theme of every sermon, the minister told of an elderly woman without much money to put in the offering. Embarrassed by her lack of means, she tried to slip two one-dollar bills into the offering plate without being noticed. Learning that she had just placed in the offering her last two dollars, a man at the church promised her that day that God was miraculously going to enable her to get her broken-down car fixed. He instructed her to take her car to the best mechanic in town, and that she wouldn't need to have any money. She did as told.

To cut a long story short, the mechanic eventually found the reason her car wasn't running well. Disconnecting one of the hoses revealed thousands of dollars secreted away in it. "You see," the preacher thundered, "a mafia don had owned the car. He didn't want anyone to find his money, so he hid it"—where all mafia dons hide their money—in a hose connected to the engine of the kind of car a little old woman might buy.

I hear such stories and see churches perfectly willing to tell their people that they have Jesus' crown of thorns on display, and I realize that Christianity is in crisis. Faith in Christ is a very simple matter: believe in God, accept Jesus as Savior, repent of your sins, and live by faith in the Son of God with the Bible as the foundation of your faith. Pretty simple.

But "honor this fake crown and you'll be blessed by God" and "send us all your money and God will bless you with plenty more" seem incongruous with the kind of Christianity

Jesus taught. Or that the apostles proclaimed. Or that people preached during the Reformation when serious, dedicated, sober representatives of God exhorted people to live godly lives of radical commitment to Jesus.

Perhaps that is why so many non-Christians can't bring themselves to have faith in God. Why many equate the Bible with fairy stories. And perhaps why the masses have no time for Jesus. A lot of serious-minded people witness what masquerades as Christianity today, and conclude, "If this is Christianity, I'm better off without it."

Some years ago Robert Murray McCheyne wrote, "Study universal holiness of life. Your whole usefulness depends on this, for your sermons last but an hour or two; your life preaches all the week. If Satan can only make a covetous minister a lover of praise, of pleasure, of good eating, he has ruined your ministry. Give yourself to prayer, and get your texts, your thoughts, your words from God. Luther spent his best three hours in prayer."

McCheyne was a Scottish Presbyterian minister who died young of illness at the age of only 29. While I'd never advocate we turn back the clock and try to relive the "good old days"—which, generally speaking, were never anywhere near as "good" as many people claim—it is easy to see that religion in general doesn't possess the same vital power as when the early Christians healed the sick, raised the dead, and prayed open prison doors.

It is hard to imagine the early Christian church venerating relics. Harder, still, to imagine Paul writing to the Galatians or the Corinthians and using unlikely-sounding stories in order to goad them into giving to his church. (Especially the Corinthians: Paul went out of his way to stress to them that he was not looking to be financially enriched at their expense.)

Today's religious emphasis appears to be—generally speaking—focused more on self than on self-surrender. We live in an entertainment age, and even in church many people look to be entertained. Sadly, many church leaders attempt to be entertainers. Something seems to be missing. Perhaps Paul put his finger on it when he said in 2 Timothy 3:5 that many during earth's last days would have "a form of godliness but denying its power."

Is what we see really how faith ought to look as people prepare for the return of Jesus? Now, before I come across as entirely negative and dismissive, let me assure you I am absolutely not. Many wonderful churches do many great things to reveal the character of Jesus, and there are a great many Christians living for God's glory.

But I talk to people frequently who tell me that even though they attended a Christian high school when they were younger, the vast majority of their former classmates are no longer remotely close to Jesus and have, in many cases, left their churches. Somehow it isn't the least bit surprising to hear that many young people have abandoned Christianity, or that yet another pastor has left ministry in disgrace. One might ask, "But aren't pastors people too? Can't they make mistakes just like everyone else?" The answer is "Yes, they are, and yes, they can." But should they? The answer is No, they should not.[1]

I'll never forget what the officiating minister said during my ordination to the gospel ministry. "Your church has a right to expect much of you." Those words hit me like a ton of bricks. I realized he was dead right. While I always had known what he said to be true, the responsibility of God's call to ministry became very clear in that moment. "People are looking to the minister. They expect you to be a spiritual leader. It's your duty to stay close to God. And if anyone knows how that's done, it should be you!"

The bottom line is God put the church in the world to be its light. To be the salt of the earth. To be His witnesses, and to "proclaim the praises of Him who called you out of darkness into His marvelous light" (1 Peter 2:9).

So how's the church doing?

27

For reasons that may never be understood, evolutionary theory has invaded Christianity. An alarming number of Christians have chosen to believe either the theory of evolution initially popularized by Charles Darwin, or theistic evolution, the concept that suggests God used evolution as a means of developing life. As far back as 1996 no less influential a person than Pope John Paul II issued a statement supporting theistic evolution, that God used evolutionary processes during immense periods of time to accomplish the work of creating our world.

Whether intended or otherwise, such a view renders the Bible virtually meaningless. Scripture clearly states that God created the world, and that He did so in six days. The challenge of having a biblical discussion with a proponent of theistic evolution is that evolutionists do not begin with a biblical perspective. They promote a view that originates entirely outside of the Bible, with no single verse in all of Scripture even suggesting any support for their theory.

The opening verse of the Bible confidently asserts, "In the beginning God created the heavens and the earth" (Genesis 1:1). Genesis 1:27 says, "So God created man in his own image; in the image of God He created him; male and female He created them." And Psalm 33 captures the majesty and magnificence of the creation story by stating, "By the word of the Lord the heavens were made, and all the host of them by the breath of His mouth. . . . For He spoke, and it was done; He commanded, and it stood fast" (verses 6-9).

Reading those verses is not like trying to decipher the prophecies of Ezekiel or Zechariah. They are straightforward statements not open to interpretation—other than the one clearly intended. God is the architect of creation. He intentionally designed the world, as well as human beings. The Lord created in six days. He originated the human family on the sixth day of Creation week, and by creating through the power of His Word, He was not dependent on any natural processes to bring the universe into existence.

The Bible doesn't even suggest that God brought life from nonlife.

When I interviewed Ken Ham, the president of the Creation Museum in northern Kentucky, he spoke of what he regarded as the danger theistic evolution presents to the next generation of believers. Today's young people, Ham believes, are having their faith in the Bible undermined by a significant segment of the church that has rejected some of the plainest statements in the Bible.

Jesus Himself certainly did not accept theistic evolution, stating in Mark 10:6 that Adam and Eve were made at "the beginning of creation." Christ believed the story of the flood in Noah's day (Matthew 24:37), and He viewed the seventh-day Sabbath as a memorial of Creation (Mark 2:27, 28).

And all Christians recognize that the Bible teaches death originated as a consequence of human sin (Romans 5:12). Theistic evolution, however, posits that death occurred long before human beings came into existence.

Although a 2012 Gallup poll revealed that 46 percent of Americans believe in creationism, the United Methodist Church,[2] the Episcopal Church,[3] the United Church of Christ,[4] and many other denominations reject the Bible teaching on the subject of origins. And while it is no surprise that state-run high schools and colleges teach evolution as fact, even Christian high schools and colleges have taught evolutionary theory as fact, despite the fact that it directly contradicts the Bible.

And before I earn myself the label of a "Bible literalist",[5] I recognize that Scripture does have some things that we don't read literally. Much Bible prophecy is symbolic (see Daniel 7:1-8; Revelation 13:1-8; etc.). Even though Paul instructed his readers to "greet one another with a holy kiss" (Romans 16:16), I have to confess that—with the exception of my wife and children—I've kissed very few of my fellow believers. We must read the Bible in context. But while it hardly matters whether you kiss someone's cheek or warmly shake their hand, what a person believes about creation and evolution radically affect their view of the entire plan of salvation, the law of God,[6] and the reliability of the Scriptures. In other words, if we can't believe the Creation story, what in the Bible can we trust? The answer must surely be: precious little.

The largest church in the world has been embroiled in scandal for the past decade or so because of the immoral behavior of some of its priests. It's a terrible thing for a church to be defined by, and the scandal hangs over it like a dark cloud.[7] Far from pointing out the sins of the clergy of one denomination in particular, it's (sadly) necessary to mention that no church can claim to be free from moral scandal. And that's really the point. The church? The home—and sometimes the defender—of the morally bankrupt? How can that be?

The tragedy is that in many respects the church is very little different than the world. Corporately, much Christianity seems to have lost its rudder. Perhaps it has abandoned its moral compass. Today churches debate issues that those of yesteryear wouldn't have considered to be questions needing discussion. For example, entire denominations have divided over the question of the ordination of practicing homosexuals. How did this even become a topic in Christian circles?

It should be clear that homosexuality is a more complex issue than many Christians might consider it to be. Why people are gay is not an easy question to answer. Some people—for whatever reason—choose to be that way, either for a period or for a lifetime. You'll read interviews with people who say, "I decided to go down that road for a while and then realized it wasn't for me." And I've met some of those people.

Today's increasingly gay-tolerant world[8] encourages people to be open to homosexuality simply by virtue of its pervasiveness, and the media has highlighted gays and gay issues in recent years. What was once taboo is no longer so.

A high school senior told me 10 years ago that many in his school considered gays "cool," and that his school not only tolerated homosexuality but promoted it in various ways. In 2013 a suburban New York high school's yearbook featured a homosexual couple as "cutest couple."[9]

Whatever the reason a person believes himself or herself to be homosexual, there's no excuse for Christians to be hateful toward them. Jesus loved all people, regardless of their morality (see John 4:18; 8:3), and Christians today should do the same thing. But does loving someone mean that their lifestyle should not disqualify them from being church leaders? Some denominations think so. But the Bible clearly states otherwise.

This is not a question with which churches should be struggling. But many *are*. And they also struggle with other questions like it, even though God clearly does not approve of immorality.

No, we don't want to seem—or be—intolerant. Nor do we want to make it appear as though we're consigning someone to outer darkness. But what happened in the church that we can no longer confidently state that wrong is wrong?

Is the church in crisis? It would appear so. While it may not be readily apparent in the United States, church attendance has dropped precipitously in many countries, particularly developed ones. In some nations—especially in Europe—there exists an almost palpable cynicism toward organized religion. A Croatian woman I met in Berlin described herself as "a Catholic on strike." "I still like Jesus," she told me. "It's the church I'm not so sure about."

In 1966 *Time* magazine's front cover asked, "Is God Dead?" While God is certainly not dead,[10] *Newsweek* magazine's April 13, 2009, cover dealt with a similar theme: "The Decline and Fall of Christian America." A Los Angeles *Times* article in 2011 described America as "spiritually promiscuous." While celebrating a Pew Forum finding that about half of all Americans will change their religious affiliation at some stage during their life, it also stated that approximately 20 percent of American Christians believe in reincarnation, astrology, and yoga—spiritually ruinous New Age beliefs with no basis in Scripture.

A generation ago such a finding would have scandalized much of Christianity. I vividly remember the Pew findings published in 2011. Barely a whisper greeted them.

Now, it is certainly true that we find much in American churches that is good and noble and right. But we cannot escape the fact that Christianity has undergone an alarming metamorphosis in recent years. Gone are the days when truth was all that mattered and people universally proclaimed the Bible as a divine revelation of the mind and will of God. Theories and suppositions and cultural relevance have graduated from the back seat to the driver's seat. Or if they're not in the driver's seat, they're at least sitting in the passenger's seat with their hands on the steering wheel.

Pastor Shane Anderson wrote in a magazine article that in his opinion, many young Christians today live "a surprisingly stark blend of the altruistic and the hedonistic, the orthodox and the heretical." He observed that many young people in churches these days "do not sense a need to resolve their conflicted lifestyles. They may recognize their inconsistencies, and certainly some do want to get rid of them. But a surprising number do not; they are comfortable with their contradictions."

Contradictions riddle Christianity as an entity. In May of 2011 a Gallup poll revealed that 92 percent of those surveyed answered yes when asked if they believe in God. Seventy-eight percent of Americans claim to be Christian. That equals 245 million. Yet studies show that less than 18 percent of the American population regularly attends a Christian (Catholic, mainline, or evangelical) church, and that, typically, 40 to 60 percent of church members are inactive.[11] Anyone who has been a pastor (as I have) can tell you that masses of people belong to a church, say they love Jesus, claim they believe in

God, and yet rarely darken the door of the church and do not maintain a devotional life. And before we define genuine Christianity as attending church, those same pastors can tell you that an alarming number of active church members do not live remotely Christian lives.

Is the church in crisis? Oh, yes, it is. Church leaders try their best to find methods of growing their congregations. Or reviving them or reconnecting with missing members. Hence the proliferation of programs in today's churches, most of which represent a desperate attempt on the part of leadership to convince churches to do the job they were raised up to do, and to convince members to take their faith seriously.

And why is this? What's the root of the crisis that has sucked the life out of the church? It's interesting to me to hear what some people say would fix the church's woes. "If only the music was better." The music could certainly improve in many churches, but when music becomes the basis for a worshipper's experience, then we've got other problems to address. "The people aren't friendly." That's a fair point, but it's the exception, not the rule. Plenty of extremely friendly churches dot the landscape.

"The sermons are too long." "The sermons are too short." "The pastor shouldn't wear a suit and tie, but should dress down to make the visitors feel more welcome."[12] While there's always going to be a segment of the population with whom such points resonate, the fact we find thriving congregations that are traditional, that are modern, that have long sermons, short sermons, modern music, traditional music. . . .

But let me suggest a reason that the church is in crisis today. I don't mean to intimate that it is the only one, but in my mind it's key. First, read this quote from a book written more than 100 years ago—one of the most profoundly insightful and relevant volumes I've ever encountered.

"Many who call themselves Christians are mere human moralists. They have refused the gift which alone could enable them to honor Christ by representing Him to the world. The work of the Holy Spirit is to them a strange work. They are not doers of the word. The heavenly principles that distinguish those who are one with Christ from those who are one with the world have become almost indistinguishable. The professed followers of Christ are no longer a separate and peculiar people. The line of demarcation is indistinct. The people are subordinating themselves to the world, to its practices, its customs, its selfishness. The church has gone over to the world in transgression of the law, when the world should have come over to the church in obedience to the law. Daily the church is being converted to the world."[13]

This isn't rocket science, although a frightening amount of people fail to make the connection. If you develop a taste for M&M's, cauliflower isn't likely to excite you. You'll see it with young children: I've watched mothers struggle to get their infants to eat vegetables when all morning they've filled them with fruit juice and Cheez-Its. You love what you learn to love, what you develop a taste for. And if all week long a person watches Hollywood dramas and wacky comedy shows, the poor old preachers doing their best in the pulpit don't stand a chance. Sit your kids in front of cartoons all week, and they're going to have little interest in the children's Bible class. "My children are bored in church." Of course they are! Because at home they're being excited by inane, special effects-laden entertainment shows created by some of the most creative minds in the world. Church simply can't compete with that! As Paul wrote in Romans 8:7: "The carnal mind is enmity against God; for it is not subject to the law of God, nor indeed can be." The sooner people accept that fact, the better off they will be.

If I had a dollar for every time I heard some well-meaning soul say that "the church isn't doing enough for our young people," I'd be a wealthy man. But while that may be true in some cases—I'm not wanting to let the church entirely off the hook here—the fact is it isn't the church's job to save anyone's children. It never has been, and it never will be. When the parents are watching what the world does, listening to the same thing everyone else is, dressing just like those around them, there's little chance the children are going to find much to get fired up about in the book of Isaiah. So what do we do in response to today's crisis in the church? All too often we turn to entertaining our children in church because "at least they're coming."

I'm the first to recognize how difficult the challenge is. I have kids of my own, and I used to work in the entertainment industry. We're involved in a really, really big battle against a very, very experienced enemy. Revelation 12:12 says: "Woe to the inhabitants of the earth and the sea! For the devil has come down to you, having great wrath, because he knows that he has a short time." With little time left before Jesus returns, Satan has raised his game. As an expert in human psychology, he knows what buttons to push, which impressions to make, and how to draw a human heart away from the love of God.

If Satan can get us distracted enough by the world that devotion to God ceases to be a priority, and prayer and Bible reading no longer form a meaningful part of the life; if he can educate our children to believe that the Word of God doesn't really mean what it says; if he can convince teachers and parents to react against the legalism of yesteryear by relaxing standards and downplaying accountability; if he can bring us to the place where we love the world more than we do God, we're going to be stuck in sin, and too indifferent to realize that fact.

"No, Olga," I would have liked to tell those who came to adore that relic in Notre Dame Cathedral. "Jesus didn't really wear that crown. Nobody knows where the actual one is. Which is a good thing, because if they did, people would make an idol of it and treat it just like you and your fellow pilgrims did. Olga, God wants you to *think*. To make good decisions based on the Word of God, not on finite human

35

science, not on the prevailing culture, and not even on what people say in church. If you can learn to have a relationship with God based on the Word of God, Olga, Jesus will give you your own crown to wear. And it won't be long, Olga, because Jesus is coming back soon!"

Identifying the problem might not be the hardest—or most important—thing we could do. The question is: Is there a way out of where we are? The answer is definitely yes. And we're going to find out what it is.

---

[1] And yes, I am very mindful of 1 Corinthians 10:12, which says, "Let him who thinks he stands take heed lest he fall."

[2] "We find that science's descriptions of cosmological, geological, and biological evolution are not in conflict with theology."Available online at www.umc.org/site/apps/nlnet/content. aspx?c=lwL4KnN1LtH&b=5066247&c+-1-6715227.

[3] The Episcopal Church has spoken of "the glorious ability of God to create in any manner, and in this affirmation reject the rigid dogmatism of the 'Creationist' movement." Available online at www.pewforum.org/Science-and-Bioethics/Religious-Groups-Views-on-Evolution.aspx.

[4] "Evolution helps us see our faithful God in a new way. Our creator works patiently, calling forth life through complex processes spanning billions of years." Available online at www.ucc.org/not-mutually-exclusive/pdfs/pastoral-letter.pdf.

[5] And one could earn oneself far worse labels, I'm certain.

[6] If the Sabbath is a memorial of Creation (see Ezekiel 20:12, 20; Mark 2:27, 28) and Creation week never existed, there's absolutely no reason, from a biblical point of view, for anyone to keep the Sabbath.

[7] I hasten to point out that I knew many priests when I was growing up. All of them were fine men who were never known to do anything morally inappropriate. Some of us considered it odd that one of our parish priests had his own live-in housekeeper, a spirited Irish woman who was a fierce defender of the faith. But nobody ever said anything out loud about the arrangement. That wouldn't have been the proper thing.

[8] Witness NBA player Jason Collins' "coming out." The president congratulated him, Oprah hugged him, and others compared him to Jackie Robinson. And Collins was by no means the first major sports figure to come out. Others included such athletes as Martina

Navratilova and baseball player Glenn Burke (who played for the Dodgers in the World Series against the Yankees and was very open about his orientation in the mid-1970s). We should note, however, that Burke wasn't greeted with the same enthusiasm as was Jason Collins. He lasted four years in the major leagues. Ostracized and derided by many, he died of AIDS in 1995.

[9] http://abcnews.go.com/US/wireStory/cutest-couple-ny-high-school-boys-19317801#.Ua4YuLSyfzI.

[10] *Time*'s then editor, Otto Fuerbringer, died in 2008. The writer of the article, John Elson, died in 2009. God's funeral isn't expected any time soon.

[11] www.churchleaders.com/pastors/pastor-articles/139575-7-startling-facts-an-up-close-look-at-church-attendance-in-america.html.

[12] In the United States Catholic Church attendance has held stable since 1995, despite the scandals that have rocked Catholicism. And have you seen what *priests* wear to church? The minister's choice of clothing doesn't seem to bother Catholics.

[13] Ellen G. White, *Christ's Object Lessons* (Washington, D.C.: Review and Herald Pub. Assn., 1900), pp. 315, 316.

CHAPTER 3

People in Crisis

She was such a sweet woman. Although I had never seen her at church, I had visited her often at the nursing home where she lived. Just after arriving in town—and before I had moved to the area—she came down with a serious illness that at first prevented her from getting out of her house, and eventually saw her moving to a nursing home, her health failing. Since she had attended the church only once, very few of its members even knew who she was. Except for the fact that she had family in town who checked on her and visited with her often, she would otherwise have felt alone.

One day I received a letter from her. It said something like, "Pastor, please come and visit me as soon as you can. I have something very important to tell you." While I couldn't imagine what it was she had to say, somehow I sensed it probably wasn't good news. And I was right.

"So, what's going on?" I asked her after we had chatted for a few minutes.

"Well . . ." she began with a smile on her face. I always enjoyed visiting her. Relentlessly positive, she still possessed a zest for life despite her ill health. She had photos of her family proudly displayed on her walls, and yellow-headed birds dined at the feeders strategically placed outside her large windows. I wondered what was coming. The longer she paused, the more I sensed it was not going to be good news.

"Well," she began again, "the doctors say I have cancer again. Only this time I'm not going to make it."

"No?" I asked, my voice a mixture of concern and calm. "What are they saying?"

"They say I have somewhere between three and six months."

"Oh. That's not good. How do you feel about that?"

Her response almost caused me to laugh out loud. "You know, I've always tried to get cancer in a part of my body that I have two of something. I've lost a breast and then an eye. Which was OK because I had two of them. But I have only one liver."

Probably, I laughed out loud. I suppose it was not the textbook response when someone tells you they have a terminal illness, but this woman wasn't the textbook person. Ava[1] had something about her that was unique, a disposition possessed by few people I've ever met. Although perhaps it wasn't her disposition. Actually her sunniness, since her positivity ran much deeper than a disposition ever could.

"So are you going to be OK?" I asked her. I'll never forget her answer as long as I live.

Ava's life was in crisis. She was going to die. It can't get much worse than that. And even though many people— most people?—live with crises from time to time, some carry seemingly unbearable burdens.

Dr. Burl Gilliland and Dr. Richard James wrote that a crisis is "a perception or experience of an event or situation as an intolerable difficulty that exceeds the person's current resources and coping mechanisms."[2] And it isn't surprising that end-of-life issues are the source of great anguish for a lot of people.

A New York City pastor told me that the biggest questions high-powered people have are about the end of life. A man who has regular Bible studies with some of the country's most influential people told me that the topic of the Bible studies more often than not finds its way back to the question of what happens when you die. Everyone lives in the shadow of that crisis.

And it's remarkable that in this enlightened world,

the benefit of hindsight does not always help us avoid the mistakes of the past.

In the first week of September 1929 New York City was waking up from another summer of leisure, its streets crowded with back-to-school and back-to-the-city shoppers. Fifth Avenue windows drew crowds who admired the latest fashions. Theater-ticket brokers found themselves rushed; Broadway musicals had sold out months in advance. The noise of the building industry reverberated along streets and avenues as towers and terraces kept rising. And the stock market stood at an all-time high.

On the third day of September a single share of Montgomery Ward, bought for $132 the previous year, was now worth $466. Shares in Radio Corporation of America— otherwise known as RCA—which sold the previous year at $94.50, now went for $505. A lot of people in those heady days owned thousands of such shares, which was possible because one could buy them with only 10 percent down. The purchaser owed the broker the rest.

Then, on the fourth of September, a little slip occurred— not enough for anyone to really notice. The following day the New York *Times* index reported a 10-point drop in the market. Nothing terribly serious. However, Roger Babson, a well-known writer and business theorist, suggested that the wild ride of prosperity was over and that a depression was on the way. But like the warnings of many prophets— whether in sacred or secular lines—people dismissed him as an alarmist. The prevailing thought was that things always go down a little bit before the rise continues. What goes up, as they say, must invariably come down, at least for a time.

But by October 21 the slide had picked up speed, and brokers began sending out margin calls. When the money wasn't forthcoming—and how could it be?—the dumping began. On October 24—later known as Black Thursday— the structure of the market cracked wide open. Millions of shares got pitched into screaming chaos on the floor of the New York Stock Exchange. Outside the stock exchange crowds stood numbly, hoping against hope that something would reverse the terrible collapse and retrieve what they and countless others were about to lose. The day would become known as the "day of the millionaires' slaughter."

As writer George Santayana has stated: "Those who do not remember the past are condemned to repeat it." Seventy-nine years after the Great Depression began, the United States experienced the financial collapse of the fall of 2008. The housing market had caved in the previous year when people who couldn't afford to finance mortgages obtained loans from institutions that in some cases could ill-afford to lend. Easy credit, fraudulent underwriting, and predatory lending were everywhere. And as a result, people found themselves horribly vulnerable when the economy tanked. Jobs vanished, and mortgage payments became either excruciatingly difficult for many people, or simply impossible. Evictions and foreclosures multiplied, and today many people still feel the pain. Eventually the stock market—which in October 2007 had soared to record levels—dropped from its zenith of 14,000 points to a nadir of 6,600. This was a major crisis.

We are vulnerable to financial crises today. Companies have outsourced jobs by the millions as businesses seek to improve their bottom line. Entire industries such as the auto industry and the building industry, have sailed through troubled waters, leaving in their wake thousands of men and women out of work and out of hope.

It's true that economies are sometimes up and sometimes down, but the United States economy has never looked as fragile as it currently does. By May 2013 the country's national debt was close to $17 trillion, or a little more than $53,000 for every man, woman, and child in the country. And the economic pain experienced by the country as a whole means crisis levels of anxiety suffered by its citizens.

I sat one day in the lovely home of a ministerial couple

who explained to me what the failing economy had done to them. Having bought their home when the market was up, they now owed far more than it was worth. They were wondering if they should do what so many others had done: walk away from their home and let their bank own yet another property. Their debt was so large that they were certain that in the remaining years they had in the workforce they could never realistically hope to repay it. Real people, real pain. As M. Scott Peck wrote in the best-seller *The Road Less Traveled:* "Life is difficult."

And today people are doing whatever they can to deal with their difficulties. The Centers for Disease Control (CDC) and Prevention announced in 2011 that 11 percent of Americans over the age of 12 take antidepressant medication.[3] The same report states that an astonishing 23 percent of all American women in their 40s and 50s—almost one in four—are now using antidepressants.[4]

The CDC also found that almost one in five high school-aged boys in the United States have been diagnosed as having attention-deficit hyperactivity disorder (ADHD).[5] It isn't hard to believe that something is definitely amiss in the face of such statistics. The New York *Times* quoted Dr. Jerome Groopman, a professor of medicine at Harvard Medical School, as saying, "There's a tremendous push where if the kid's behavior is thought to be 'abnormal'—if they're not sitting quietly at their desk—that's pathological, instead of just childhood."

Once when I was on a plane I sat next to a man who served on the board of a summer camp, the same one he had attended when he was a child. Today he is a tremendously successful businessman, having run major corporations in the United States. I was interested in something he told me. He said that when he attended summer camp 50 years ago, a child might once in a while have to take an aspirin. When his own children were in the same summer camp 25 years ago, he noticed the occasional child who needed medication for one thing or another. Being on the board of the summer camp enables him to know that today fully 50 percent of the children arrive at camp with a medication regimen.

The issue of anxiety and depression is enormous, and represents not only a national crisis but also personal crises. I've seen it firsthand on our *It Is Written* television program. Viewer response following two interview programs with Dr. Neil Nedley, author of *Proof Positive* and the developer of the Nedley Depression Recovery Program, was higher than for any other *It Is Written* television segment I can remember. Far higher. We live in a stressed-out world, and people are struggling to cope.

The personal struggles many are experiencing are taking a heavy toll on the family. It is said that the divorce rate among Christians is similar to the general population's.[6] While many people would save their marriage and preserve their family if they could—often finding themselves embroiled in a situation through no fault of their own—the fact is still that divorce is often destructive and hurtful. Children frequently find themselves the victims of the poor choices of one or both of their parents, or of the parents' inability to resolve their conflicts. The high divorce rate reflects poorly on the church. One would be excused for thinking that if a couple had *God* to go to—the omnipotent Maker and Savior of the universe—they ought to be able to find a way to mend their differences and refloat their sinking relationship.[7] But all too frequently that's just not the case. The United States averages a divorce every 13 seconds.

And with this in mind, the future isn't looking too bright. In 2009, 41 percent of all births were to unmarried mothers. Children born to unmarried mothers have greater chances of growing up in single-parent households, living in poverty, and suffering from emotional problems.[8] They will more likely achieve lower grades than children born to married mothers, typically engage in sex at a younger age, and then themselves have children born outside of marriage. Later in life, children born to unmarried mothers generally earn less, do not have as good jobs, and are more likely to themselves experience marital troubles and divorce. And that's where we are today.[9] Thankfully, birth outside of marriage doesn't automatically guarantee a troubled or less-privileged future. Many people who found themselves in such a situation have gone on to do extraordinarily well. Often mothers outside the traditional marital arrangement do a remarkable job of raising their children. But the statistics demonstrate it is far from the ideal situation.

So what is a person to do who finds themselves in a crisis? Where can one turn when life is tough, the family is failing, stress is high, and the economy is fragile?

President John F. Kennedy once said, "When written in Chinese, the word 'crisis' is composed of two characters. One represents danger, and the other represents opportunity."[10] To express the thought in a similar way, we could state that humanity's extremity is God's opportunity. That is to say, every difficulty provides an opportunity for God to show His grace and power.

When a crisis appears in our lives—whether it be financial, medical, spiritual, relational, or emotional—that's a very direct call to us to turn to God. Sadly, though, that often is the only time many seek Him. Far better to be connected to God at all times so that when difficulties present themselves it will be as natural to go to God as when a flower faces the sun at midday.

In Psalm 50:15 God says, "Call upon Me in the day of trouble; I will deliver you, and you shall glorify Me." That sounds like a guarantee to me. If it was the only such statement in the Bible, perhaps we could regard it skeptically. But it's one of dozens in which the God of the universe promises His companionship, guidance, and protection.

The Lord said to His people in Isaiah 41:10: "Fear not, for I am with you; be not dismayed, for I am your God. I will strengthen you, yes, I will help you, I will uphold you with My righteous right hand." And Jesus said to His disciples, "Lo, I am with you always, even to the end of the age" (Matthew 28:20).

God's promise is that He will be with those who call on Him, those who love Him, those who choose to trust Him—which is not to say that God is some kind of cosmic Santa Claus, handing out the very presents we asked for at exactly the time we expect them. Believing in God requires a certain level of maturity, a trust that extends beyond gifts and handouts, and is prepared to have confidence in Him even in times of trouble and confusion.

A friend of mine was diagnosed with cancer as a teenager. Months in the hospital and the very best of medical care could do nothing to ward off the disease, and the hospital released her so that she could die at home. Learning of her illness, members of a local Christian congregation asked her parents if they could take her to church to pray with her. The day after the prayer meeting the young woman felt better. Before long she was certain she had been healed. When her astonished doctor encountered her on a city street some weeks later, the physician invited her to undergo testing at the hospital's expense. Today, decades later, she is perfectly well and cancer-free. Her miraculous recovery has only one explanation: God intervened and healed her.

On the other hand, we all know people who have been gravely ill and trusted in God that He would heal them. And they are the ones whose graves we visit and whose memories we treasure. Clearly faith in God isn't a "Get Out of Jail Free" card we can redeem at any time.

The seeming randomness of God's providence perplexes many people. After a natural disaster or some other terrible event that results in senseless loss of life, we find Internet message boards filled with predictable comments: "Where was your God when the bomb went off?" and "If God was as good as you say, why didn't He save those people from dying?"

In 2007 one of the most remarkable stories ever to emerge from New York City unfolded at the 137th Street/ City College subway station. A 20-year-old man suffered a seizure on the station platform and fell onto the tracks in the path of an oncoming train. A construction worker named Wesley Autrey climbed down onto the tracks, intending to lift Cameron Hollopeter up onto the platform. But with a train rapidly approaching, Mr. Autrey did not have time to perform the rescue. Instead, he did something even more heroic.

Quickly sizing up the depth of the drainage trench between the tracks, Mr. Autrey figured there was room enough for him to lie on top of Hollopeter and hold him safely in place while the train rushed over both of them. His experience in working in confined spaces paid off. The trench had just enough room for the two men, but it was tight enough that Autrey ended up with grease marks on the cap he was wearing—grease marks made by the train as it passed over him and the man he saved.

A believer would most likely say, "That was God's doing! God saved the men!" Which actually raises a difficult issue. If God saved Cameron Hollopeter and Wesley Autrey, why did He not save Ki-Suck Han when a homeless man pushed him into the path of an approaching train at the 49th Street/ Seventh Avenue station shortly before Christmas in 2012?

Is God's role in a time of crisis merely to provide checks in the mail, job offers at the perfect moment, and miracle cures from heart disease or depression? Perhaps several Bible stories offer some clarity.

In the hours before Jesus died He found Himself nailed to a cross (as Isaiah 53:12 predicted), with a criminal on each side of Him. Initially the thieves hurled abuse at Him, but one of them—possibly deeply impressed by Jesus' demeanor as He endured crucifixion—not only rebuked his fellow criminal but implored, "Lord, remember me when You come into Your kingdom." And Jesus answered, "Assuredly, I say to you, today you will be with Me in Paradise" (Luke 23:42, 43).[11] He promised the thief the gift of salvation.

But Jesus didn't miraculously release the thief from the cross and his indescribable agony. Crucifixion was a brutal, horrible way to die, calculated to be especially painful. The very best that Jesus could do for the thief was to assure him that beyond his miserable death on the cross, eternity would stretch before him. The man's legs would still have to be broken, he would have to endure a ghastly death from asphyxiation, and he would die a condemned thief—not any kind of reformed, rehabilitated hero. Nobody in Jerusalem that day would have remembered him as anything other than a condemned thief. His association with Jesus did not release him from the terribleness of crucifixion. But knowing Christ offered him hope, hope beyond his present situation.

Is that the perfect Christian cop-out? "No, God didn't heal your son, Mrs. Smith, but at least you can be glad that you'll see him in heaven." One could see it that way. Or we could rather understand it as a manifestation of God's goodness and mercy. As Paul wrote in Romans 14:8: "Therefore, whether we live or die, we are the Lord's." The fact is that what happens to us during our earthly sojourn is ultimately of little consequence. What matters is where we spend eternity, and how we employ our time on earth in preparation for the life to come. Jesus summed up the thought by saying, "What will it profit a man if he gains the whole world, and loses his own soul?" (Mark 8:36).

Peter was imprisoned when an angel woke him up, caused his chains to fall off, and escorted him past the guards—even reminding him to put on his sandals and bring his cloak (Acts 12:6-10). This came as such a shock to the church that when a girl named Rhoda told the believers that Peter was outside the house, they instead thought she was out of her mind.

And why were they so certain it couldn't be Peter? Because earlier in the same chapter James had been executed at the command of King Herod. The believers were certain the same fate awaited Peter.

So why was Peter saved and James allowed to die? That's not a question anyone can answer with certainty, other than to say God allowed what He knew to be best according to His divine wisdom. The issue isn't about God's fairness—or lack thereof—in the way He handled the cases of Peter and James. The question is one that people have struggled down through the ages. Of Abraham concerning Isaac, of the spies concerning the Promised Land, and of Daniel in the lions' den. Are you prepared to trust God no matter what? Can you have confidence in Him, even when things look bleak?

As the disciples were sailing one night across the Sea of Galilee, a storm rose that threatened to sink their vessel. They woke the sleeping Jesus, desperately appealing to Him to do something about their extremity. "Lord, save us! We are perishing!" (Matthew 8:25). The disciples were panicking, while Jesus was sleeping through it all.

Jesus commanded the wind and the waves to be still, demonstrating that He can do one of two things when events shake our lives. He can calm the storm, or He can keep us calm in the midst of the storm.

God doesn't always remove the crisis. In fact, if you read the Bible's book of Revelation you'll see that history's greatest crisis is still ahead. But the Lord has shown that He has the capacity to divide seas, feed people in a desert, open the eyes of the blind, make people impervious to flames, raise the dead . . . Such are the things He can accomplish when He chooses to do them. But when He decides otherwise, and the consequences aren't what we would normally wish for, God is still God! He is still good, and He is still love (1 John 4:8). When we find ourselves in the midst of a crisis, we can know that God is with us, feeling our pain and providing comfort and strength.

Standing in Ava's room in that nursing home, I looked at my elderly friend with real affection. She was going to die. Yes, miracles still happen, but she was resigned to facing the toughest challenge she had ever had. There wouldn't be surgical intervention or chemotherapy. Ava was going to die. There's nothing very easy about that.

I put my hand on her. "Are you going to be OK?"

She smiled. "You know what?" I shook my head. "I'm going to be fine. Me and Jesus are going to get through this together!"

And they did. Death followed the timetable outlined by the physicians. Her funeral was a thing of joy and remembrance. She navigated her final days with grace and dignity, and died surrounded by her family.

Hers was not a paper cross. A terminal illness is a crisis. But Jesus helped her bear the load. He was with her at every stage of her tremendous challenge. She and Jesus got through it together.

Ava could still be alive today. People have lived much longer. Why did God not allow her the blessing of good health, the joy of her family and friends? I suppose we'll find out one day. Or perhaps when we get to heaven we quite possibly won't want to know. It's as likely as anything else that the thought won't enter our heads. And why? Because we'll be with God. We'll be in heaven in the presence of the angels and the redeemed of all ages. God will be glorified. And nothing else will really matter.

Jesus never did promise us a life devoid of crises. In John 16:33 He said, "In the world you will have tribulation; but be of good cheer, I have overcome the world."

Be of good cheer. In difficulty, be of good cheer. In crisis, be of good cheer. Trust God anyway. And you and Jesus will get through it together.

---

[1] Not her real name.

[2] R. K. James and B. E. Gilliland, *Crisis Intervention Strategies* (Pacific Grove, Pa.: Brook/Cole, 2001).

[3] www.cdc.gov/nchs/data/databriefs/db76.htm.

[4] While some would consider it positive that so many people

receive treatment for depression, others see the increased use of psychoactive drugs as ominous. Available online at www.nybooks.com/articles/archives/2011/jun/23/epidemic-mental-illness-why/.

[5] www.nytimes.com/2013/04/01/health/more-diagnoses-of-hyperactivity-causing-concern.html?_r=0.

[6] Opponents of that statement will say that the divorce rate among "serious" Christians is much lower than that of the general population. Thus, one could argue that the church is doing a very good job. But if the church is filled with noncommitted, unconsecrated people, could it mean that it has done well in embracing the worldly and the secular? That could be suggested. But it would be a poor argument.

[7] According to the Barna research organization, more born-again Christians get divorced than atheists and agnostics. Available online at www.barna.org/barna-update/article/15-familykids/42-new-marriage-and-divorce-statistics-released.

[8] www.childtrends.org/?indicators=births-to-unmarried-women#_edn19.

[9] Please understand that I'm not being critical of people who find themselves in this situation. Statistics need not define a person's life.

[10] As inspiring as President Kennedy's words were, it is unfortunate for authors and public speakers everywhere that some linguists say his interpretation of the Chinese language is incorrect. At best, they admit, President Kennedy's interpretation is a stretch.

[11] Note: The thief did not go to heaven with Jesus that day, although the punctuation in verse 43 leads one to the implication that he did. (Punctuation marks were a later addition to the scriptural writings.) Jesus Himself didn't go there for another couple days. Notice His statement to Mary Magdalene in John 20:17: "Do not cling to Me, for I have not yet ascended to My Father." Neither did the thief ask to go to heaven with Jesus that very day. "Remember me when You come into Your kingdom" was his appeal. Jesus has not yet come into His kingdom. That will happen at the Second Advent—still a future event.

CHAPTER 4

Trusting
in a Time of Crisis

I thought it was a remarkable thing for someone to declare, "My husband's illness is the very best thing that has ever happened to us." She was sitting right next to him as she said it.

As a pastor visiting in a church member's home, you don't want to look too surprised at whatever someone says, no matter how startling it might be. As though I heard things like this every day, I calmly asked, "Really?"

"Absolutely." Then she went on to explain why.

The illness she was referring to was no small thing. If he had had a bad cold or pneumonia or even a heart attack and was now on the road to recovery, I could easily understand what she meant. I read about a man who was playing a game when one of his opponents punched him in the head. The next day, his head still hurting, he visited a doctor, who discovered that he had a serious medical condition that medicine could treat. Without that blow, the man wouldn't have known about his illness and may well have died. This was the best thing that ever happened to him; it saved his life.

But this was different. Her husband had a form of incurable cancer. The physicians had given him six months to live. That was six years ago. While he was still a sick man, and while life presented some real challenges, he was not only very much alive, but his extended life meant he was able to be involved in raising his young son. And best of all, he had found hope in Jesus. His illness had caused his family to reassess their priorities, to decide what was really important in life, and to make the changes they felt necessary for their family to be truly Christian. And that was why the young wife and mother was able to call her husband's illness "the very best thing that has ever happened to us."

When faced with a crisis, a person might react in countless different ways. It isn't unusual for people whose world is falling apart to turn their backs on God, believing their calamity is evidence that He doesn't care. In his acclaimed book *Night* holocaust survivor Elie Wiesel quotes a despairing Polish rabbi exclaiming in anguish, "It's over. God is no longer with us.... Where is God's mercy? Where's God? How can I believe, how can anyone believe in this God of Mercy?"[1]

Even the faith of the prophet Elijah found itself seriously shaken when the wicked queen Jezebel threatened him. And consider the context of the episode: Earlier Elijah had received food from ravens, worked miracles on behalf of the widow of Zarephath, raised the woman's son from the dead, and witnessed God send fire from heaven on the top of Mount Carmel.[2] Yet when a messenger brought to Elijah a death threat from the Phoenician princess, Elijah's default reaction was not to remember how the providence of God had so remarkably protected him up to that point. The Bible doesn't record that Elijah fell to his knees and begged for God's mercy and grace. The prophet simply fled.

In fact, he was so despondent that he wanted to die. First Kings 19:4 says that Elijah "prayed that he might die, and said, 'It is enough! Now, Lord, take my life.'" Crises even cause great individuals of faith to lose sight of God's goodness. James 5:17 reminds us that "Elijah was a man with a nature like ours." And at times that nature doesn't hold up well under pressure.

Others react to crises by attempting to compensate in some other area of their life. People frequently turn to alcohol or drugs as an escape, as a way out of their current difficulties. Some find refuge in food, others in hedonism, still others in misdirected intimacy. And it isn't unusual for people dealing with crises to spend money as a way of forgetting their woes.

A New Zealand couple made the news after their plans to check things off their bucket list took an unexpected turn. Diagnosed with terminal cancer, the 69-year-old man along with his 65-year-old wife, decided to spend his last days doing the things he had always wanted to do.

They sold their home at a substantial loss, canceled their health insurance, and enjoyed international travel staying in five-star resorts. The husband resumed smoking cigarettes and drinking coffee, things he had quit during his first cancer scare. They gave away $30,000 worth of tools, and invested in a business. After visiting their daughter and grandchildren, they returned to their hometown and waited for the husband to die.

Instead, almost two years later, with his health showing no signs of decline, further testing revealed that he did not, in fact, have cancer, and that the earlier diagnosis was a mistake. While happy he was not terminally ill, the couple were conflicted about their current situation. Their spending spree had left them $80,000 in debt. Even their business venture had failed.

But then there's Job. When a series of tragic events robbed him of not only his possessions but also his 10 children, he responded by saying, "Naked I came from my mother's womb, and naked shall I return there. The Lord gave, and the Lord has taken away; blessed be the name of the Lord" (Job 1:21).

Confident that a more significant crisis would cause Job to abandon his faith in God, Satan challenged the Lord by declaring, "Stretch out Your hand now, and touch his bone and his flesh, and he will surely curse You to Your face!" (Job 2:5). So God gave Satan permission to afflict the man physically, and Job began to suffer from a hideous disease that left him in constant miserable pain. Job 2:7 records that "Satan went out from the presence of the Lord, and struck

Job with painful boils from the sole of his foot to the crown of his head." The man's physical condition was so serious that even his wife urged him to "curse God and die!" (verse 9). And the friends who visited him in his distress offered him nothing in the way of support or consolation.

Yet in all of this Job's response was that of faith and trust. It doesn't mean that he didn't have his moments of darkness. But he was able to say in Job 13:15, "Though He slay me, yet will I trust Him."

And therein lies the key. Job was able to trust God, no matter the circumstances. How was it that he was able to develop that incredible level of trust?

While in New York City recently, I noticed as I walked along the street where I was staying in the Hell's Kitchen neighborhood a man attempting to get his bicycle in through the door of his apartment building. It was a wet day, he was wrestling with what appeared to be a couple bags, and my impulse was to stop and help him. "Hey, buddy, I'll hold your bike here while you get that door open and put your bags inside." But then it occurred to me that this was New York City, and I was a perfect stranger. Would the guy even trust me? Or would he be suspicious of my motives? I couldn't expect him to trust someone he didn't know and had never even seen before.

You'll see a similar thing when traveling by plane. A young mother struggles aboard the aircraft with two or more small, wriggly children while doing battle with a diaper bag, her carry-on bag, her handbag, a teddy bear, and a car seat. My wife has often offered to help in such situations, and always gets welcomed with a grateful smile and kind words of thanks. When traveling alone I have offered to help in similar situations. And at times I've been met with a stoic look and "No, thank you. I'm fine." The trust level just isn't there.

So how can you trust someone enough so that even when a crisis strikes you can move forward securely?

I heard about a woman who after some major testing learned that she had only weeks to live. Her reaction startled the medical staff. She raised her eyebrows, nodded her head, and said simply, "H'mmm." Thanking the staff for their time, she stood to leave the room. They stared at her, amazed. And a little worried.

"It isn't often that we see a person deal with news like this so calmly," a doctor said. "Is everything OK?"

"Yes, everything's OK," she answered. "This isn't the news I was hoping for, but if God has allowed this to happen, then I can trust that somehow He has a plan for me."

Now, I don't mean to intimate that the only right way to handle a crisis is with stolid impassivity or quiet resignation. Sometimes there might be tears, sometimes desperation. The suffering Jesus experienced on Calvary caused Him to cry out, "My God, My God, why have You forsaken Me?" (Matthew 27:46). But as He hung on that cross, Jesus was able to trust His Father completely. He had said the night before, "O My Father, if it is possible, let this cup pass from Me; nevertheless, not as I will, but as You will" (Matthew 26:39), and just before He died He told God, "Into Your hands I commit My spirit" (Luke 23:46). Like Job, Jesus was able to trust His Father, believing that His Father's plan would ultimately work out for the best.

What are the things that actually cause anxiety in a person's life? I once read that someone estimated that 70 percent of what people worry about will either never happen or can't be changed. I can't say with certainty whether those figures are entirely accurate, but as many people reflect upon the causes of their consternation they often discover little or no basis for their worries. While many people do face incredible challenges, it is also true that humans are highly skilled at creating crises out of little or nothing.

But what if you knew Someone who was able to get you out of—or get you through—any crisis life could throw at you? What if there was someone you could trust totally and completely, Someone who had enough wisdom, enough energy, enough money and relationship skills to help you deal with *any* situation?

I heard recently from a friend who explained that she and her mother are "not close." Sadly, many people can relate to that. But then there are those whose parents are their best friends and closest confidants. Parents who shower their children with love and patience have raised their kids to trust them completely. Whereas some of us would say, "I could never talk to my mother/father/parents about *that*," others confidently announce, "I can talk to my parents about *anything*."

The difference usually results from bonds formed through time spent together. Family vacations, hikes in the woods, volleyball games, family bike rides, meals eaten together . . . When a family takes time together, and if relationships are healthy, its members usually have a level of trust and respect that makes for positive relationships.

Time. Time spent together. Combine that with love and mutual respect, and that's what makes the difference. In the same way, when we get to know God we learn that we can trust Him to help us through the most difficult of crises. It fascinates me that so many people dismiss God as being distant or aloof, out of touch with our daily cares and concerns.[3] Many have portrayed Him as intolerant and hateful. But look at what God says about Himself, and ask yourself if this is the sort of person who might be able to help you when things aren't going right in your life: "For I know the thoughts that I think toward you, says the Lord, thoughts of peace and not of evil, to give you a future and a hope" (Jeremiah 29:11).

That remarkable statement declares that He has only the best intentions toward our world. And taken in context, God uttered those words to a people about to go through a terrible crisis. The nation of Babylon would soon take Israel captive. For seven decades God's children would be prisoners in another country, stripped of their independence and robbed of their autonomy. And yet God tells this rebellious, stubborn nation that His thoughts for them are to give them hope and prepare for them a viable, vibrant future.

Think back to earth's original crisis. When God created the world, He placed our original parents in the midst of a beautiful garden. Giving them authority over the entire Garden of Eden, He had only one caveat: "Don't eat the fruit that grows on the tree of the knowledge of good and evil" (see Genesis 2). He told them what the consequences of disobedience would be—death—and even explained what the issue was: that of "good and evil."

God had described creation as "very good." It seems hard to imagine He didn't explain to Adam and Eve the meaning of the word "good." As limited as their understanding had to have been in that early age, they undoubtedly knew God's will on the matter of eating the fruit, and that to do so would be a serious matter with deadly results.

But consider the situation from God's point of view. Eating the fruit wouldn't only have deadly consequences for Adam and Eve and the entire human family. Disobedience on their part would seriously affect heaven itself! Should they sin, Jesus would have to die. He was "the Lamb slain from the foundation of the world" (Revelation 13:8). That is, before the creation of the world the Godhead had decided that in the event of sin, Jesus would die as a sacrifice for the fallen human race.

The sin of Adam and Eve meant that they would have to forfeit their lives. Not simply because of divine displeasure, but as the inevitable result of the effects of sin. The prophet Isaiah wrote in Isaiah 59:2 that sin separates a person from God. Life is only found in Christ (1 John 5:12), and those who do not possess Jesus by faith are disconnected from the source of all life—the original Life-giver (John 1:3). The break that now existed between Adam and Eve and their Maker meant that they would ultimately perish.

But God had a plan! What if He were to offer Himself in place of Adam and Eve? What if Jesus, the divine Son of God, died instead of them? True, the degradation that now existed as the result of sin would before long claim their physical lives, but if Jesus were to take their punishment—and being the Law-giver, His death would satisfy the claims of the law—then Adam and Eve have another chance at life. Only this time, they would have to depend totally on Jesus to receive the help they would need to overcome their now sin-tainted nature. Left to themselves, they would degrade. As water naturally flows downhill, sinful people would naturally follow their sinful tendencies. But with Jesus' help, they could live holy lives in preparation for eternity.

Simply put, when Adam and Eve sinned, they signed Jesus' death warrant. Put yourself in the place of His Father! The two people He had made were about to cost Him His Son—the Son He had known and loved from all eternity past. If you were in God's place, what would your reaction be?

The Bible's best-known verse states that "God so loved the world that He gave His only begotten Son, that whoever believes in Him should not perish but have everlasting life" (John 3:16). When Adam and Eve sinned, God—who could have destroyed them both without anyone questioning His right to do so—instead chose to manifest love, because "God is love" (1 John 4:8).

While we read or hear of numerous instances of people forgiving someone who murdered their family members, I don't recall a single instance in which a relative of the deceased offered to suffer the death penalty in the place of the guilty murderer.

But that's exactly what Jesus did. And He didn't give Himself to die for a world full of sorry, repentant, broken-hearted people. The Bible says Jesus was "despised and rejected by men" (Isaiah 53:3). John wrote that "He came to His own, and His own did not receive Him" (John 1:11).

Instead of welcoming their Messiah, Israel shunned the One whom heaven had sent to save and prosper them. The religious establishment not only dismissed Him but plotted to kill Him.[4]

Paul wrote that "God demonstrates His own love toward us, in that while we were still sinners, Christ died for us" (Romans 5:8). And after they ate the fruit, how did God react toward Adam and Eve?

He pursued them. Not in order to punish them or berate them or humiliate them, but so that He could win them back to Himself. As they hid from God in the Garden of Eden, wearing fig leaves in order to hide their now-embarrassing nakedness, they heard the "sound of the Lord God walking in the garden" (Genesis 3:8).

What would the Lord say to the two rebels? Their selfish actions had plunged the world into sin and had opened the floodgates to misery and sadness and hardship and evil. And worst of all, now Jesus would have to die. But what God told Adam and Eve is nothing short of amazing.

"Then the Lord God called to Adam and said to him, 'Where are you?'" (Genesis 3:9). Either God had lost Adam and Eve—highly unlikely—or He was revealing to the universe the depths of divine love. "Adam, where are you?" The Lord was not asking Adam and Eve where they were *geographically*. Your GPS might have tried to drive you through houses or dead-end streets, but God's is in perfect working order. He was asking Adam and Eve where they were *spiritually*. They had wandered from Him, and He was asking them if they realized they had done so, if they had any awareness of the seriousness of their situation.

That is how God deals with a crisis. He pours Himself into our lives at infinite cost to Himself. Humanity creates a disaster, and God willingly steps in to provide a solution and a way out for His wayward children. As Abraham told Isaac in faith, "God will provide for Himself the lamb for a burnt offering" (Genesis 22:8). We mess up, God cleans up. We fall over, God picks us up. We rack up a debt we could never repay, God takes care of it.

So let me ask you: Is this the kind of Deity you could trust in a crisis?

God has never shown Himself to be anything other than entirely trustworthy. While it is difficult to comprehend that while we're in the midst of a crisis, it is easy to see in retrospect. In other words, if you can't see God's leading right now, you're likely to be able to become aware of it as you later look back on a situation.

A young wife might initially think God has abandoned her family when a serious illness strikes her husband, but she can come to the place where she sees God's hand and recognizes He is still present in her home and life.

Israel could not comprehend that going into Babylonian captivity could be anything but a complete disaster. It isn't hard to understand why they might think that way. But in Jeremiah 25:9 God described the Babylonian king Nebuchanezzar as "My servant." The Lord would use Nebuchadnezzar to accomplish His purposes of purifying Israel and helping them to choose the service of righteousness rather than that of sin.

Remember the Polish rabbi quoted by Elie Wiesel in his book *Night*? He couldn't see it from his vantage point at the time, but the fact was that evil was not going to triumph. It had its day in Auschwitz, but would not ultimately be victorious.[5]

In 1990 a 19-year-old American student was a passenger in a bus hit by a runaway truck in Jerusalem. He was airlifted to the United States with a broken neck, his future forever altered. A journalist today, he described in an article on CNN.com how he returned to Israel 22 years after the accident to meet with the other survivors of the crash and see how the incident had shaped their lives—or how their lives had affected their view of the collision and its results.[6]

Many of the survivors of the accident viewed it as being

God's will—even if they could not entirely understand it. The driver of the runaway truck stated the crash was an act of God, using an Arabic word to describe the whole event: *Maktoob* (It is written). That is, whatever happens, God knows ahead of time, taken by many to mean that certain things are preordained, destined to happen according to divine will.

But the journalist was not satisfied with that version of events. He considered the location of the accident—a dangerous bend, the site of 144 accidents with casualties during a span of 30 years. Furthermore, he noted that the driver of the truck had been driving carelessly and was habitually a dangerous driver. And he identified certain other factors that undoubtedly directly contributed to the disability with which he now lives.

The author stated that he is now agnostic in his views about God. (Agnostics believe that God is essentially unknowable.) Unable to see a bigger picture, unable to perceive any purpose in the tragedy that befell him, unable to comprehend how the saving purposes of a loving God could reveal themselves in a random act that inexorably altered his life, he chose to believe what so many others have: "This makes so little sense that the idea of a loving, sovereign God also makes no sense." And that's the greater tragedy.

Consider: For God to prevent every crisis from occurring, He would constantly have to intervene to prevent the outworking of our ability to exercise freedom of choice. The Lord could have stopped Adam and Eve from eating the forbidden fruit, but then without the power to determine their own course they would be robots and not people. God wouldn't be a Deity of love. Instead, He would be a God of manipulation. A dictator. The Lord allowed Adam and Eve to make choices for themselves. Even when those decisions were bad ones and would cost God more than they would anyone else.

The cross demonstrates the love of God in the midst of

61

a crisis-filled world. Our sin—so destructive that it causes eternal death—was of such concern to God that He chose to allow Jesus to die in our place rather than to see us helplessly suffer the full effects of what we had brought upon ourselves. By hanging on the cross, Jesus said, "Can you see how much God loves you and cares for you? Can you discern how much He wants for you to have hope and a future? Your sin was *so* bad that the only way you could sin and still have access to heaven was for Me to die for you. And as indescribably high that price is, heaven was willing to pay it. Why? Because God is love."

So whom would you trust in a crisis? It might be difficult to have confidence in God, because the One—the only One—who had the ability to prevent your situation chose not to do so. And now you're in a fix—or in a wheelchair or a hospital bed—because God chose not to intervene. But balance those thoughts with what the Bible tells us about God's love, His constant care and perfect love, and the promise of everlasting life in a land where there will be no crises, and perhaps we *can* then put our complete confidence in Him. Trust isn't always easy. It can sometimes be messy. But to do so with God in the midst of a crisis provides certainty, security, and a future filled with blessing and joy.

In 2005 a panicking 30-year-old New York woman faced a terrifying choice: that she and her 3-week-old son would somehow survive the fire engulfing their third-floor apartment, or to throw her son from the apartment in the hope that someone below would catch him.

Thinking *It's either me or my baby,* and praying that someone would be below, Tracinda Foxe released her son and felt him fall from her grasp.

New York Housing Authority supervisor Felix Vasquez happened to be in the right place at the right time. Mr. Vasquez—the catcher for his Housing Authority baseball team—caught the falling baby and performed mouth-to-mouth resuscitation. The infant—who had not been breathing when he landed in Mr. Vasquez's arms—started to cry. Fire department workers looked after the child and rescued the desperate mother.

Tracinda dropped her baby from a third-floor window in the hope that *someone*—a stranger, someone she had never met—would save him from the crisis that had swept over them both. Remarkably, he landed unharmed, saved from what might otherwise have been certain death.

Sometimes crises demand that we take a leap of faith. Except that any leap God calls on you to make is not a jump into the unknown. In a time of crisis the God who promises to catch you[7] is a deity you know—or can know—from experience. Someone in whom you can have complete, unreserved trust.

If God is calling you to take a leap of faith, you can jump into His arms knowing He will never let you fall. Even if it doesn't look that way at first.

---

[1] In Elie Wiesel, *Night* (New York: Hill and Wang, 2006), pp. 76, 77.

[2] Read the dramatic stories in 1 Kings 17 and 18.

[3] Read the comments on Internet message boards. While not representative of the entire population, they demonstrate that a lot of people haven't "friended" God.

[4] His own church plotted to kill Him! See John 11:49-53.

[5] That's something I took away from visiting Auschwitz: evil doesn't triumph. Ultimately, goodness wins. And that's very true of the great spiritual conflict we find ourselves in the midst of. Evil does not win—love wins. *God* wins!

[6] www.cnn.com/2013/05/22/opinion/prager-our-suffering-gods-will/index.html?hpt=hp_t4.

[7] See Isaiah 41:10. The thought is very similar.

CHAPTER 5

Promises You Can Trust

An American couple on their way to Africa were surprised to find themselves traveling in entirely the wrong direction. Intending to fly from Los Angeles to Dakar (the capital of Senegal, the West African country that borders Mauritania to the north and Guinea and Guinea-Bissau to the south), they connected to a flight in Istanbul, Turkey, that they believed would take them to Dakar. But they were surprised to see the aircraft's in-flight map reveal that they were flying above the Middle East, the wrong direction if your intended destination is West Africa.

Owing to a mix-up with airport codes, the couple had instead taken a flight to Dhaka, Bangladesh, rather than to Dakar, Senegal. Hearing the flight attendant say "Dhaka" during preflight announcements didn't help them avoid confusion, as they mistook "Dhaka" for "Dakar." They had sat back to enjoy what they thought was the final leg of their journey, but their trust in the airline's ability to get them where they wanted to go soon received a serious dent.

What reason do you have to think that God can get you to where you want to go? Interestingly, He has given us evidence after evidence to demonstrate that we can have total faith and trust in Him. And He has done so in a way that allows us to put Him to the test.

Thousands of years ago God inspired the writing of the Bible. Beginning with Moses—who prepared the first five books of the Bible and the book of Job—and ending with John, who composed the book of Revelation,[1] "holy men of God spoke as they were moved by the Holy Spirit" (2 Peter

1:21). God did not dictate the Bible to human beings to write down word for God-spoken word, but He moved upon them by the power of the Holy Spirit and inspired them to write—in their own words—the thoughts and ideas that He impressed upon them.

But in some portions of the Bible God did speak directly. At times people did hear God's voice, and the biblical authors did record what He said for posterity. The New Testament contains the words of Jesus, and God Himself wrote the Ten Commandments (see Exodus 31:18).

In the Bible God puts Himself on the line as no other religious figure has ever done. He repeatedly makes predictions, claims about Himself, and promises to His people that are verifiable, and—frankly—either true or false.

One thing I've always wondered is why more people don't study the Bible. That is, if what it says is true, then the vast majority of people on the earth might well find themselves on the wrong side of God's will on the day of judgment. And if, as the Bible says, a glorious eternity stretches ahead of us, wouldn't everyone want to know if they can be part of that?

The Nigerian e-mail scams that became so ruinously popular around the turn of the present century cost a lot of people a lot of money precisely because they thought, *This could be too good to miss out on!* They sent bank details to complete strangers who cleaned them out financially simply because "if this is true, I don't want to miss out on it."

I recall speaking to a detective about a woman who had apparently squandered large sums of other people's money. She had been in touch with "a man" who had told her that if she sent him a little money it would unlock for her a vast sum that someone had set aside in her name. Convinced she was on the verge of a fortune, she sent the money, only to be informed to send more. And then more. And each time she dutifully obliged. Until she ran out of money.

That was when she convinced others that a wonderful investment opportunity awaited them. If they would give her $5,000, $10,000, $15,000, that investment would be multiplied exponentially, and together they would all have more money than they could ever wish to have. In the end, a lot of people lost a lot of money, and detectives found themselves wondering what to do about a dear old lady who had made a series of terrible—and costly—mistakes.

People ordinarily want to have that which is "too good to be true." When the jackpot in the Powerball lottery got up to $590 million in May 2013, people who normally didn't buy lottery tickets joined with others to swell the jackpot to near-record highs. A spokeswoman for the Arizona lottery described the interest in it as a "complete frenzy" on the day the lottery numbers would be drawn. Observers in Louisiana described lottery fever there in much the same way. In the end, a single winner bought a $2 ticket that brought a prize of well more than a half billion dollars,[2] at odds of one in 175 million—the largest single Powerball payout in history.

Now let's consider that. Odds of one in 175 million. Nationalgeographic.com reports that the odds of lightning striking the average American in any given year are one in 700,000. An American who lives to be 80 years old faces odds of being hit by lightning of one in 3,000.[3] It is said that an amateur golfer has an almost one in 13,000 chance of hitting a hole in one, and a more than one in 67 million chance of scoring two holes in one in the same round.

If you made a round-trip flight every workday for 30 years, your chances of dying in a plane crash are one in 787. The odds of a woman naturally conceiving quadruplets are about one in 730,000.

A couple has a 230 times better chance of naturally conceiving quadruplets than winning the Powerball lottery, but millions of people buy lottery tickets "just in case."[4] Because, well, you never know. And that's true. Someone has to win.

But all the money in the world can't compare to what the Bible promises. It speaks of forgiveness, the removal of guilt and condemnation, a place forever in the heart of the infinite God, and the gift of eternal life in a perfect world. And eternity is a very long time.[5]

So what if it's true? Wouldn't a person want to know? Even if it's "just in case"?

One of the most remarkable things the Bible quotes God as having said appears in Isaiah 46:9, 10: "Remember the former things of old, for I am God, and there is no other; I am God, and there is none like Me, declaring the end from the beginning, and from ancient times things that are not yet done."

God claims that He has the ability to foretell the future. And it must be that He either does or He does not. Can we verify it? Is God telling the truth here? Let's find out.

In Daniel 2 Nebuchadnezzar, the king of Babylon, had a dream so impressive that it woke him up. Unable to recall it, though, and desperately wanting to do so, he summoned his counselors to tell him what he had dreamed and what it had meant.

When they failed, the king sentenced them to death. Daniel—absent from the meeting with the king but also considered one of the king's "wise men"—requested time to interpret the king's dream. After God answered his prayer for insight, Daniel explained to the king that what he saw was an impressive statue made of four different metals: gold, silver, bronze, and iron.

The Hebrew prophet explained to the king that the statue's head of gold represented Nebuchadnezzar's kingdom of Babylon. Then Daniel said, "But after you shall arise another kingdom inferior to yours" (Daniel 2:39). Quite the thing for him to say, and very courageous considering to whom he was speaking. Daniel was telling the king that his kingdom would one day be conquered, which—considering the might of Babylon—was almost a preposterous thing to claim.

Babylon was located in the area of the world known as

the Fertile Crescent, in what we would today call Iraq, and it had an intricate system of canals that irrigated lush croplands. It was famed for the Hanging Gardens of Babylon, one of the Seven Wonders of the Ancient World. The walls and roof of Babylon's main temple were plated with gold, while the altar and throne were solid gold. But this magnificent kingdom would collapse into the hands of another power.

And Daniel went on to say that the kingdom that conquered Babylon would itself fall to another kingdom that would in turn be taken over. Then, changing tack, the prophet did not predict that the fourth kingdom would be conquered. He said instead that it would unravel, fall apart, and divide rather than be overthrown.

History demonstrates that Daniel's prediction—or, more accurately, God's Word—met its fulfillment in every last detail. The combined kingdom of Medo-Persia conquered Babylon. Greece, led by Alexander the Great, overwhelmed the Medo-Persians. And then Rome took over Greece. But Rome wasn't conquered by anyone, except perhaps by itself. Beset by infighting and immorality, the empire split into numerous entities after repeated attacks from various barbarian tribes.

During World War II some Bible preachers conducted large public meetings that they advertised by saying, "The Bible Says Hitler Can't Possibly Win the War." One could call their advertising strategy risky, or one could describe it as the safest in the world. Rather than making a prediction of their own, those lecturers were simply quoting what God had already said, and what history had proven to be true.

Now, surely God could have simply been lucky with the prediction. Or Daniel could have made a good guess. Or the Bible writers might have written the book of Daniel long after those events had taken place. But rather than regarding the book of Daniel with skepticism, Jesus trusted its prophecies to be reliable, as attested to in Matthew 24:15.

Certainly, if that was the only prediction God aced, we

could have reason to believe He was something of a one-hit wonder, a spiritual Starland Vocal Band[6] who got lucky once and otherwise did nothing to suggest prophetic reliability.

But this is God we're discussing here. Christianity would never have gotten off the ground if He had not been able to keep His word.

Consider some of the other remarkable predictions God made—each of which came to pass.

In Genesis 6:13-17 the Lord predicted a flood would deluge the earth. Genesis 7:12 records that it rained for 40 days and 40 nights, bringing destruction to the Earth according to the Word of God. (Keep in mind that up until that point, it had never rained on the earth.)

In Joshua 6:26 God spoke through Joshua and said that whoever tried to rebuild the ruined city of Jericho would lose both his eldest and youngest sons during construction. Then in 1 Kings 16:34 we read that a man named Hiel attempted to rebuild Jericho, and that both his firstborn and his youngest sons died during the construction process, just as God had said would happen.

In Jeremiah 25:11 the prophet stated that Israel would go into captivity in Babylon for 70 years, another prophecy precisely fulfilled.

Micah 5:2 predicted Jesus would be born in Bethlehem, 700 or so years before the event took place. Zechariah 9:9 states that He would ride into Jerusalem on a donkey. Both Matthew 21:5 and John 12:15 record the fulfillment.

Daniel predicted not only the year of Jesus' baptism (Daniel 9:25) but that of Jesus' crucifixion (verse 27). Isaiah foretold that the Messiah would be born of a virgin (Isaiah 7:14), Isaiah 53 describes how those He came to save would reject Him, while Psalm 22 dramatically describes the manner of His death.

Jesus Himself predicted His own death and betrayal, and even that one of His closest friends would deny any connection to Him (Matthew 26:2, 21, 34).

Now, if this is all we had—God's ability to predict future events—it would provide us with, at best, some measure of comfort. But what would it matter if God could predict the future but wasn't interested in our present? That is: What is it a person needs during a crisis? A predictor of events? The God of the Bible has revealed Himself to be far more than a foreteller of the future.

In demonstrating that He knows the future of the world, God displays not only His divinity but also His trustworthiness. If we can have confidence in what He tells us about the future, then undoubtedly we can rely on the rest of what He says in the Bible. And so much of what He presents is designed especially to give us confidence in the midst of crisis.

God knew the world would be spinning apart as the twenty-first century wore on. He foresaw the heartache people would experience. Massive financial problems don't take Him by surprise. God knew that Ponzi schemes would rise long before anyone had ever heard of Charles Ponzi. He saw people rebuilding their lives after tornado or hurricane devastation, and knew that disease epidemics and war would keep breaking out; and, having demonstrated that He can talk about the future, God can with authority speak to people dealing with shattered lives and broken dreams.

And consider what God does. He makes *promises*. And as He has demonstrated—consistently and repeatedly—that what He predicts invariably comes to pass, we can surely believe the promises He makes to us in the Bible.

So what about God's promises? Unlike those made by human beings, they will never fail. They cannot. The Bible says, "God is not a man, that He should lie" (Numbers 23:19). Do you recall what happened when Moses went up to the summit of Mount Sinai to receive the Ten Commandments from God? The people had said to him, "All that the Lord has spoken we will do" (Exodus 19:8). However, before Moses could make it down from the mountaintop, the Israelites had fashioned a golden calf and were worshipping it—in violation of God's will, and contrary to their own sincerely made vow.

Was there anything wrong with the promise made by the children of Israel? No, inasmuch as it expressed the right sentiment. But yes, in that human beings are notoriously bad promise keepers.

But what God pledges *will happen*. And if we understand this, we'll never face another crisis without the complete confidence in His ability and willingness to guide and bless.

The Bible contains literally hundreds of promises. Let's look at a few of them and see how they can make a difference in your life. It won't be difficult to think of situations where they can have a huge impact.

Hebrews 13:5 records that Jesus said, "I will never leave you nor forsake you." When the world—or when your world—looks as though it is coming apart is precisely the time you want to remember this promise. God has said that He will never leave you. He's with you. You are not alone. The One who wrapped the rings around Saturn has told you that He cares for you, which means there's no reason for you to wonder, worry, or doubt. God has said it, you can believe it, and that's that.

Once I spoke with a woman who asked me if God would forgive her for a sin that she had committed. I assured her He would. "But, Pastor John," she persisted, "it's a terrible sin."

"That's no problem for God," I replied. "He's in the business of forgiving terrible sins." And then I asked her, "Have you confessed your sin?"

"Yes, many times." She told me that the thing had happened 50 years ago and that she had confessed it every day, sometimes many times a day. "Why," I replied, "that's more than 18,000 times!"

"Yep, that's about right," she agreed.

So I asked her if she believed God. "Yes, of course I do."

"Well, based on what you're telling me, you don't believe

God at all," I continued. "In fact, you believe He is a liar."

Then I opened the Bible to 1 John 1:9, and read to her, "'If we confess our sins, He is faithful and just to forgive us our sins.' Have you done that?" I asked her.

"Yes, I've done that" came her timid reply.

"All right, so 'if we confess our sins, He is faithful and just to forgive us our sins and to cleanse us from all unrighteousness.' Does God tell the truth?"

"Yes."

"All the time?"

"Yes, I believe so."

"Well, here God is telling you that He forgives you. And if He has forgiven you, why in the world would you go back to Him and confess again, as though you don't believe the promise He has made to you?" I encouraged her to believe God's simple, powerful promise to her and not give this thing another thought. And when I saw her next, she told me that that night she'd had the sleep she'd not had in 50 years.

Job loss, money worries, no food in the pantry, a car in need of repair, healing from an illness, a new suit for church or work . . . life is full of needs. And needs are different from wants. You *want* a Bentley, but you *need* a way to get to work. While you may *want* a million dollars, you *need* a way to pay the rent. God understands that we have needs. And He acknowledges that in one of the most comprehensive promises found in the Bible.

Philippians 4:19 says, "My God shall supply all your need according to His riches in glory by Christ Jesus." And that's a promise. You can take it to God just as you would a check to the bank, and you can expect Him to provide what He has promised.

Will He really do that? Yes, He will. Then, if I need a car, He'll give me a car? Well, let's be careful here. God knows our needs, and He will meet them. You might figure you require a car, yet God provides you with a ride to work courtesy of a kind neighbor. Or you might think you must have money to pay the rent, when what God knows is that being evicted is going to get you out of a bad neighborhood or help you avoid some terrible future situation. God knows best. And when we accept that, we won't look at His promises the way children do the list of Christmas wishes they hand Santa Claus in a department store. We present God's promises to Him, believe that He hears, know what He has promised, and trust Him to do what is best in a given situation.

For the person who is experiencing a spiritual crisis, God made a promise that is filled with meaning and possibility. And the fact is, many, many people are undergoing spiritual hardship. Sometimes it's the very ones who look as if they have got it all figured out who are having the hardest time. A person who knows all the answers, who grasps the theory of a relationship with God, who is familiar with the Bible and yet continues to experience spiritual failure, often can easily feel as though they've let down God so badly that He is done with them.

But read this promise: "No temptation has overtaken you except such as is common to man; but God is faithful, who will not allow you to be tempted beyond what you are able, but with the temptation will also make the way of escape, that you may be able to bear it" (1 Corinthians 10:13).

"God . . . will not allow you to be tempted beyond what you are able." When a friend offers me a drink or drugs, or when I'm tempted by immoral behavior, the biblical truth is that I'm not doomed to fail. Temptation can be successfully endured, because God has promised that He will give us a way of escape. And that way of escape is . . . Jesus. When temptation comes we can call on Him, and He will deliver us.

"But you just don't know how tough it is," you might protest. Maybe I don't, but I know Jesus and how tough *He* is. And that's all I need to know

Jude 24 says, "Now unto Him who that is able to keep you from falling" (KJV). So if you've been visiting the wrong kind of Web sites, or if you've not been able to keep out of bars, God says that *He* can keep you from falling. That's His promise to you. James wrote in James 4:7, "Resist the devil and he will flee from you."

You see, when God has promised something, we can count on it. So when He declares that He's going to forgive your sins, you can afford to believe that. Or when He tells us that He will be with us in a dark time, we can trust that He will be there, as He said He will be. And when He says that He will provide for us, we can afford to trust that He will do that in a perfect way.

In the book of Malachi, God promises us that when we tithe and give offerings He will open up the windows of heaven and pour out so much blessing that we won't have room enough to receive it. Stewardship is a real challenge for those who feel as if they can't afford to give God a tenth of their income, and offerings besides. Or for people who simply don't feel disposed to cut God into their material blessings. But He has promised to bless those who are faithful to Him.

"'Bring all the tithes into the storehouse, that there may be food in My house, and try Me now in this,' says the Lord of hosts, 'If I will not open for you the windows of heaven and pour out for you such blessing that there will not be room enough to receive it'" (Malachi 3:10). Notice what God said: "Try Me now in this." Put me to the test! When we're faithful to God, He is faithful to us. In fact, He is always faithful. It is often our lack of faithfulness that prevents Him from doing more for us than He does.

One of the best books I've ever read that touches on this subject is a little volume titled *Steps to Christ*. I want to share a passage with you from it.

"You desire to give yourself to Him, but you are weak in moral power, in slavery to doubt, and controlled by the habits of your life of sin. Your promises and resolutions are like ropes of sand. You cannot control your thoughts, your impulses, your affections. The knowledge of your broken promises and forfeited pledges weakens your confidence in your own sincerity, and causes you to feel that God cannot accept you; but you need not despair. What you need to understand is the true force of the will. This is the governing power in the nature of man, the power of decision, or of choice. Everything depends on the right action of the will. The power of choice God has given to men; it is theirs to exercise. You cannot change your heart, you cannot of yourself give to God its affections; but you can *choose* to serve Him. You can give Him your will; He will then work in you to will and to do according to His good pleasure. Thus your whole nature will be brought under the control of the Spirit of Christ; your affections will be centered upon Him, your thoughts will be in harmony with Him."[7]

Isn't that encouraging? If you'll give God your will, He will work in your life.

One mistake a lot of people commit is that they make promises to God: "I'll never use a bad word again." "That's the last time I'll ever visit that Web site." And in the vast majority of cases, our promises to God are no better than the one the children of Israel offered just before they fashioned the golden calf.

The truth is that God doesn't even want us to make promises to Him. He really doesn't. Instead, He wants us to believe His promises to us. When we claim them, we'll see God do great things in our lives.

Concentration camp survivor Corrie ten Boom is quoted as having said, "When I try, I fail. When I trust, He succeeds." I read that she encouraged people to "let God's promises shine on your problems." She knew by experience what it was to experience crisis, and she learned that God was always faithful to be with her in her most trying times.

After a devastating tornado flattened parts of the Oklahoma City area in May 2013, news outlets released a home video taken by a family as they emerged from the ruins of their home immediately after the tornado had passed. The footage showed the storm system still visible in the distance, and as the family came out of what was once their home they were greeted not only by their own desperate situation, but by an entire neighborhood demolished by the deadly twister.

Houses all around their own would need to be completely rebuilt. Families now had no place to stay and would have to reconstruct their lives from scratch. After soberly surveying their altered landscape, the voice of what sounded like the man of the home said, "The Lord giveth, and the Lord taketh away."

No hint of anger in his voice, no trace of invective, no indication that he felt unfairly singled out or despondent about what had just happened. Instead, he expressed what sounded like trust, a resignation that what had happened could not be undone, and that God's goodness and blessing would be seen in their situation. Somehow.

Can God be trusted to lead? It might sometimes seem as though you're in Dhaka and not Dakar, but trust in God will see Him demonstrate to you His unfailing faithfulness.

---

[1] He also wrote the gospel of John, 1 John, 2 John, and 3 John.

[2] If the winner were to opt for a lump-sum payout, he or she would receive about $370 million.

[3] ABC news reported a 20-year-old Colombian man struck by lightning four times!

[4] One comedian was quoted as saying that if you want to simulate playing the Powerball lottery in your home, take a $1 bill and flush it down the toilet.

[5] When one of my brothers turned 50 and I wished him all the best for the next 50 years, he told me that the first 50 had gone past him "in the blink of an eye." The older I get, the better eternity sounds.

[6] The Starland Vocal Band was one of the biggest musical sensations of 1976, winning the Best New Artist Grammy Award in 1977. And that was it for the Starland Vocal Band. Gone, and largely forgotten.

[7] Ellen G. White, *Steps to Christ* (Mountain View, Calif.: Pacific Press Pub. Assn., 1956), p. 47.

CHAPTER 6

Spiritual Superman?

"Faster than a speeding bullet! More powerful than a locomotive! Able to leap tall buildings in a single bound!"

Created as a comic book character in the 1930s, Superman went on to become an American cultural icon, the subject of radio and television programs and full-length feature movies. Unless stymied by kryptonite, there wasn't anything Superman couldn't do. And while most of us realized early in life that we'd never be like him, many people find themselves in a spiritual crisis because they've somehow concluded that they have to be a kind of spiritual superman or superwoman.

Now, the fact is that Jesus did tell the woman taken in adultery to "go and sin no more" (John 8:11). Peter urged us to "abstain from fleshly lusts" (1 Peter 2:11), writing in the same book that "as He who called you is holy, you also be holy in all your conduct" (1 Peter 1:15). So in actuality our goal, our aim—God's will for our lives—is holiness. Sanctification. But it's hard to feel terribly holy when it's so easy to see your spiritual weaknesses and failings.

What is the solution to our seemingly constant spiritual failing? "Other people seem to have it all figured out," you might conclude. "They look so holy in church, always know just what and what not to say, and appear as if they're the most sanctified people that ever lived. But as for me . . ."

One thing it pays to remember is that most people aren't as perfect as you give them credit for being. An absolute truth is that we're all fallen humans pressing "toward the

77

goal for the prize of the upward call of God in Christ Jesus" (Philippians 3:14).

Does God want us to live holy lives? Yes, He most certainly does. Although you don't have to go far to find someone who'll express a different point of view, I've heard it expressed that God simply wants us to do our best.

Apart from that being a disastrously works-oriented approach to Christianity—"just do your best!"—it totally misrepresents the way God operates in the plan of salvation. Salvation has never been a matter of what we do for God. Just check with the children of Israel we discussed in the previous chapter. In their sincerity they promised that "all that the Lord has spoken we will do" (Exodus 19:8). But it was only a matter of a few short weeks after they made their grand promise to God that Moses found them dancing around a golden calf "unrestrained" (Exodus 32:25).

Did they not mean what they said when they made their vow to God? Yes, they did. Were they simply hypocrites who had no intention of obeying God? No, they had every intention of doing so.

So what happened?

The children of Israel were in the process of learning that God doesn't even want us to make promises to Him. Instead, He desires that we believe His promises to us! There's a huge difference. And if we understand that, it will revolutionize our lives.

Thanks to the unfortunate decision made by our original parents, we inherited from them a fallen, sinful nature. We are born bent to evil. Our inclination tends toward selfishness just as water runs downhill. Sin and selfishness come easy. And there's only one remedy for that sin and selfishness: Jesus.

The solution for your anger problem isn't trying harder not to lose your temper. The way to deal with your drinking problem isn't to pour all your alcohol down the drain (although that's a very good thing to do, and could be a very important part of the overall process). And the way to overcome lust isn't to throw away your computer. That may help with certain things, but it isn't a *remedy*. The cure for lust, or for any other sin, is Jesus.

The antidote for sin and selfishness is not commandment keeping. Obedience to God isn't the remedy for a wayward life. It never has been, and it never will be.[1]

In Romans 7 the apostle Paul described the struggle of anyone who is not connected to Jesus. He stated that he found himself powerless to do the things he wanted to do, and unable to live the way God desired him to live. Bitter experience had taught him that "in me (that is, in my flesh) nothing good dwells; for to will is present with me, but how to perform what is good I do not find" (Romans 7:18).

At one time in his life Paul had desperately wanted to do that which was right in the sight of God, but was completely unable to live the way the Lord intended for him.

In Romans 7:24 he asks a truly important question: "Who will deliver me from this body of death?" The answer he gives is profoundly simple, yet unfathomably powerful: "I thank God—through Jesus Christ our Lord!" (verse 25).

Paul recognized that the solution to his constant spiritual failing was *Jesus*. It wasn't "trying harder." All of the apostle's "trying harder" simply revealed his weakness and spiritual corruption.

Have you ever thought that you were spiritually weak? If so, then there's good news for you. You're in just the position you need to be in order to be saved through Jesus Christ.

Paul relates in 2 Corinthians 12:9 that the Lord told him that God's strength is "made perfect in weakness." What God did for Paul He will also do for you. The Lord filled Paul with His presence, and as the apostle surrendered to Him, the Spirit of God took over the apostle's life, consuming his weakness by the strength of God.

Before we can be healthy Christians we must recognize that we are weak and that God is strong. Jesus explained to the Pharisees that "those who are well have no need of a physician, but those who are sick" (Matthew 9:12). Those who think they're OK and fail to see their need can't possibly receive the grace of God. It comes to the weak only as they acknowledge their great spiritual need.

I remember reading a comment many years ago that King Solomon was never stronger than when he said, "I am a little child; I do not know how to go out or come in" (1 Kings 3:7). When we recognize that God came to save the weak and the erring, and that He wishes to unite His strength with our weakness, we're on the way to experiencing spiritual victory instead of spiritual failure.

It's also vital that we accept the fact that the Christian experience is a growth process. Pine trees can reach maturity in 20 years or so, but in a storm they can snap and suffer terrible damage. An oak tree, on the other hand, typically takes a lot longer to mature, but it is better equipped at handling the rigors of a storm. While as believers in Jesus we may wish to grow overnight, the reality is that a character that can successfully face the tests of this life takes time to develop.

Think about this from a practical perspective. A person comes to Jesus from living a life of sin. Having sincerely accepted Christ and having been forgiven of his or her sins, that individual is now a saved believer and has received from Jesus the gift of salvation.

But let's be honest. Is he or she likely to be the complete Christian package? No, no more than a baby has full human potential five minutes after birth. Infant Christians undoubtedly have a whole lot of growing to do, and more than likely a slew of bad habits to overcome. Or to put it another way: they will more than likely have sinful practices that they will want to put away.

But does that make the baby believer any less a Christian? Not in any way. As he or she grows, learns more of God's Word, and experiences more of the power of His presence in their life, the old life is going to be consumed in the new life granted by Jesus. As Paul wrote to the Corinthians: "Therefore, if anyone is in Christ, he is a new creation; old things have passed away; behold, all things have become new" (2 Corinthians 5:17).

As a person draws closer to Jesus, sinful habits will disappear from their life just as dead leaves fall from a tree in the autumn. The key is that the individual is *growing*, continually advancing in the Christian life.

Jesus addressed this very thing. "And He said, 'The kingdom of God is as if a man should scatter seed on the ground, and should sleep by night and rise by day, and the seed should sprout and grow, he himself does not know how. For the earth yields crops by itself: first the blade, then the head, after that the full grain in the head. But when the grain ripens, immediately he puts in the sickle, because the harvest has come'" (Mark 4:26-29).

Oddly enough, a seed planted in the ground is worth both very little and a great deal to the farmer. The moment farmers sow seed, they can no longer eat it. They cannot dig it up and sell it at the market. Nor can they process it and turn it into a variety of products. Such seed is good for absolutely nothing except for one thing—growth.

While the seed is of little "present" value, it has enormous worth owing to what it promises! As it grows and develops it will get closer and closer to being exactly what the farmer both needs and desires.

Think of corn growing in a field. When you put the seed into the ground, nothing visible happens. Someone without any knowledge of horticulture would think the farmer had just wasted his or her seed by pressing it into the soil. Several days later the nonfarmer would be completely convinced that the farmer had done a crazy thing. It appears the farmer has realized nothing from his or her investment. But before long, that corn seed will sprout and then poke its head up through the soil. At first it will be nothing more than a barely visible thread of green.

Can you eat the corn at that stage? No. Sell it? Process it? No, and no. So what is the corn good for? Should the farmer simply dig it up and throw it away? Of course he'd be foolish to do that. The farmer wants the corn to stay right where it is, knowing that with the proper care those tiny threads of green will become food on the table and money in the bank.

When the corn is several weeks along, and the ears of corn have begun developing, is it now worth anything to the farmer? Well, it can't be eaten or sold or processed. Nor can it be given away or even used for animal feed. But the farmer—or the household gardener, whichever the case may be—knows just what to do. Leave the corn to grow and develop, and wait for the big day: harvesttime.

Even though the corn is good for little during the process, even though it can't be eaten or sold for money, the corn is just where it ought to be at every stage of development.

We can use the same analogy with regard to people. A newborn baby isn't good for much except making messes and noise. Small children can't so much as tie their shoelaces or brush their own hair. A 10-year-old can't drive a car or climb Mount Everest, and even a teenager isn't going to be the head of a college department or the president of the United States.

And that's perfectly OK. I know from experience that even though a baby can't answer the phone or cook breakfast for the family, the infant is doing exactly what he or she is supposed to do: growing! Under the right conditions, provided with love and care and food and rest and everything else, that child is going to develop to his or her full potential in the fullness of time. Ditto for the Christian.

Christians, like cabbages and kids and cats and cantaloupe, must *grow* to maturity. And understanding this is vital for a number of reasons.

First, I've met a huge number of people who despair that they aren't where they ought to be spiritually. "I love God, and I pray and read my Bible, but I just seem to be such a failure as a Christian." Well, that could be because the individual is indeed a failure as a Christian. Or it could be because the person in question is still growing as a believer!

Another reason a correct understanding of Christian growth is important is that it is imperative to understand salvation is not performance-based. It is *faith*-based. While we grow as Christians we continue to exercise faith in Jesus Christ as our Savior and as our righteousness. Our goodness comes from Him. When we accept Jesus, we mature in grace toward His kingdom, becoming more like Him as our surrender to Him is more and more complete. And at every stage of our growth we can have the assurance that we are His children and that salvation is a reality in our lives.

That is certainly not to say that we should feel complacent with our failings and shortcomings. People with wicked tempers shouldn't be satisfied until they have fully surrendered to Christ and reflect Him in attitude and action. The covetous individual shouldn't feel comfortable lusting after what isn't theirs. The prideful person should know that pride is an abomination to God, bringing pain to His heart. But in all of this we must know and believe that God is merciful and gracious.

The book of Hebrews tells us that we may "come boldly to the throne of grace, that we may obtain mercy and find grace to help in time of need" (Hebrews 4:16). John wrote to his readers that they "may not sin." But he added that "if anyone sins, we have an Advocate with the Father, Jesus Christ the righteous" (1 John 2:1). Isn't that fascinating? God is not excusing sin in any way, but in recognizing its existence as well as the reality of Christian growth, He is assuring us that God's love is still extended toward us in our imperfection, and His grace is constantly on offer to the repentant, believing soul.

David wrote in the book of Psalms words similarly encouraging. "The steps of a good man are ordered by the Lord, and He delights in his way. Though he fall, he shall not be utterly cast down; for the Lord upholds him with His hand" (Psalm 37:23, 24).

A reality check might also be in order. I'm not suggesting that growing in the grace of God is an easy thing. *Theoretically* it is simple. We accept Jesus, we grow, we become more like Him, and during that process—as we are turned toward Him by faith—we have total assurance of salvation. But in practice it can be anything but easy.

I've heard it said that all the sinner needs to do is to "just trust in Jesus, and Jesus will do it all!" While that sort of statement certainly contains a germ of truth, my honest conviction is that such an attitude produces Christians who end up either extremely frustrated or extremely out of balance.

Take the example of a drinker. Upon accepting Christ, they stop drinking, and honestly trust in Jesus. It is true that in some cases even the very desire for alcohol disappears and the drinker never has to worry again about it. But a more common scenario is that from time to time—especially early in a person's Christian walk—the temptation to consume alcohol will be incredibly strong. On a hot summer's day a former drinker can imagine how a cold beer would feel and taste, and temptation begins to do its work. Similarly, the reality is that a person who has lived an immoral lifestyle might at some time or another feel strongly drawn back into it—on at least a temporary basis.

Is that evidence that a person's Christianity is not real? No, it is not. Or is that person failing for experiencing the temptation to return to their old life? Perhaps, and perhaps not. Should someone start daydreaming about how much they'd love to go back to their old life and live it up, and they allow that daydreaming to overtake them, then yes, there's something wrong. But temptation is just temptation. If a person is experiencing temptation, it is evidence of nothing more than the reality of the devil. For the purpose of this discussion, we'll give the individual the benefit of the doubt. Remember, James wrote that temptation and sin are two altogether different things (see James 1:14, 15). It isn't a sin to be tempted.

So what should a person do when temptation comes? James gave us magnificent counsel when he advised us to "submit to God" and "resist the devil," adding the wonderful assurance that when we do those things Satan will "flee from" us (James 4:7).

As an example, we'll go back to the drinker we were just considering. Their walking route home from work takes them past what was once their favorite bar, and they feel the desire to go in and buy a drink. But they remember the verse that says they should "resist the devil and he will flee from you." So our drinker does just that, and resists the devil.

You can talk all day long about what Jesus is going to do for a person in that situation, but few are the times He has actually *forced* a person to pass a bar without going inside. Instead, honoring our freedom of choice, Jesus allows us to decide what we will do. Of course, angels are there to help us and the Holy Spirit's power is extended to us, but the choice to keep walking or to turn into the bar is ours alone to make. Should the drinker choose to enter the bar, God will not force that individual not to do so. He will appeal and plead and strongly impress them to go on by, but if the drinker chooses to ignore God's appeals, the Lord will honor their freedom of choice.

However, if they yield their will to God and follow the impressions made by God to continue past the bar, former drinkers will remain former drinkers. God will empower them to get past the bar without caving in to the desire to drink. (And on a practical level, the victorious former drinker might want to choose to head home from work following another route!)

You can take that scenario and transpose it into any situation you want to. When we yield our will to God and accept His strength and power, He can help us to rise out of the muck of sin and live a new life in Christ.

Writing to the Corinthians, Paul uses an incredibly hopeful phrase: "And such were some of you" (1 Corinthians 6:11). If you read the passage, you find that he says the following just before he writes that powerful little phrase: "Do you not know that the unrighteous will not inherit the kingdom of God? Do not be deceived. Neither fornicators, nor idolaters, nor adulterers, nor homosexuals, nor sodomites, nor thieves, nor covetous, nor drunkards, nor revilers, nor extortioners will inherit the kingdom of God" (verses 9, 10).

It seems as though the apostle didn't leave a single stone unturned. It isn't easy to think of a single sin that doesn't fit into one of the categories Paul listed in the passage above. But after so clearly describing the people that will not enter into heaven, Paul writes, "and such were some of you." In other words, there are some people who aren't going to be saved. You *used to be* like that.

He goes on to add, "But you were washed, but you were sanctified, but you were justified in the name of the Lord Jesus and by the Spirit of our God" (verse 11). Having been cleansed and pardoned by Jesus, they have continued to grow in the grace of God and to experience the power of His presence. "Such *were* some of you." Although sinners of the worst kind, God's amazing grace had redeemed and transformed them.

I read an insightful article by Malcolm Gladwell titled "How David Beats Goliath."[2] What Gladwell presented in it has a strong relationship with a person's Christian experience. He quoted research conducted by a political scientist who had examined every war in the past 200 years in which one of the warring sides was at least 10 times stronger than its opponent. Surprisingly, the strong side won in only 71.5 percent of the wars in question. Even in these extremely lopsided contests, the big guy lost almost a third of the time.

What's even more remarkable is that when the little guy did two simple things, the results were staggeringly different. When the smaller, evidently weaker side recognized its limitations and then chose an unconventional strategy in the war, its winning percentage rose from 28.5 to 63.6 percent. Gladwell pointed out that when the underdog chooses not to play by the other side's rules, it wins, even when everything we know about power says it shouldn't.

The author cited the example of T. E. Lawrence (Lawrence of Arabia), who was victorious against the Ottoman army even though his own force appeared totally out of its depth. But while they couldn't be stronger than their adversaries, they could be smarter, more agile, and more aggressive.

An interesting example Gladwell used was that of a basketball team of mostly 12-year-old girls in California's Silicon Valley. An immigrant from India—a man who had never played basketball in his life—coached them. Most of the girls weren't tall, they weren't good, and they had little experience in the game. But the coach studied how people played basketball and made an interesting observation.

He noticed that basketball teams tend to follow a certain pattern. The team with the ball makes its way down the court and encounters little more than token resistance. The opposition runs back on defense to guard the area around the basket. Which means that Team A has the opportunity to approach almost all the way to the basket, thus making it relatively easy to shoot and, therefore, score.

Realizing that his team had little chance of ever winning if they allowed stronger, better teams to take the ball up the court virtually unopposed, the new coach decided to adopt an unconventional strategy. He encouraged them to press the other team all game long. When the opposing team inbounded the ball, he would have multiple players vigorously defending their counterpart, thus flustering their opponents.

And it worked! They won game after game as the teams they played had no answer for such an unusual approach to the game of basketball. In fact, the Silicon Valley team was so successful with their unconventional strategy that they went all the way to the national championships.

Recognizing their weakness led them to adopt an unorthodox strategy. And like Lawrence of Arabia's men, they had no quit in them. They would run all game long and stick to their plan.[3]

David's victory over Goliath followed this same outline. Realizing that in a straight fight he had no chance of defeating Goliath, David adopted an unconventional approach. By the end of a day of real crisis for God's people, he had won a decisive victory for Israel.

You might feel as though your foe is too big for you to defeat. Or you might have recognized that you're not a spiritual superman or superwoman. But that does not have to discourage you. God's strength is made perfect in weakness. If you can recognize your weakness and adopt an unconventional strategy, you're going to experience victory.

And what would that strategy be? A total reliance not on yourself, but on God. A firm belief that He hears and answers prayer, an entire dependence on the Word of God as the foundation of your life, and a desire that Jesus Himself would live His life in you.

The words of the old hymn put it well:

"Prone to wander, Lord, I feel it, prone to leave the God I love;

Here's my heart—O, take and seal it; seal it for Thy courts above."[4]

---

[1] If for some reason you think I'm downplaying the importance of obedience, let me assure you I'm definitely not doing so. Keep reading!

[2] www.newyorker.com/reporting/2009/05/11/090511fa_fact_gladwell.

[3] Something else that helped: the coach noticed that most other basketball coaches habitually yelled at their players. He said it was his experience that shouting at 12-year-old girls was counterproductive, so he remained calm while pacing the sidelines.

[4] Robert Robinson, "Come, Thou Fount of Every Blessing," *The Seventh-day Adventist Hymnal* (Washington, D.C.: Review and Herald Pub. Assn., 1985), no. 334.

CHAPTER 7

Facing the Final Crisis
With Confidence

A uschwitz is not a place that's easy to forget.
I've been there twice. Once to film an *It Is Written*
television program, and once with a tour group. Both visits
had about them an almost surreal quality.

The reproduction of the entrance into the Auschwitz
concentration camp—above which hang the words "Arbeit
Macht Frei" ("Work Makes You Free")—is smaller than I
expected. The halls and buildings are clean and well-kept,
sanitized. The pleasantness of a warm spring day can almost
cause you to forget that Auschwitz was a place of abject horror.
The bitter chill of a cold, snowy day jolts you into a realization
that living conditions at Auschwitz were bitterly difficult.

At Birkenau—a sister camp to Auschwitz located less
than two miles away—your blood easily runs cold in your
veins. Whereas Auschwitz was a concentration camp,
Birkenau was an extermination site. Trainloads of prisoners
would arrive at the railway platform in Birkenau, "selection"[1]
would take place, and often within less than an hour the
prisoners would be dead and cremated.

Remnants of actual gas chambers and crematoria remain
at both Auschwitz I and Auschwitz II—Birkenau. The sheer,
inhuman brutality of Auschwitz and other similar places is
virtually impossible to fathom.

The museum official who accompanied me when we
filmed at Auschwitz told me that even working at Auschwitz
can take its toll on people. The experience of constantly
reliving the appalling crimes committed there causes some
people to become depressed and hopeless.

It is chilling that Auschwitz is not the only example of large-scale inhumanity we have in recent world history. Between 100,000 and 500,000 perished in Uganda in the 1970s during the rule of former Ugandan president Idi Amin. During the three years in the 1970s that Pol Pot led the Khmer Rouge in Cambodia as the prime minister of Democratic Kampuchea, between 1 million and 3 million people lost their lives. And the Rwandan genocide in 1994 slaughtered at least a half million people.

And none of this is ancient history. All of these massive atrocities occurred in *modern* times. We can add to them the unthinkable crimes of terrorism, still holding the world in its grip of fear and anxiety. In spite of all we have learned, in spite of advanced education and decades of peace plans and international treaties, it seems human beings haven't learned from the mistakes of the past. And it appears we're doomed to repeat them.

According to the Bible, the worst is still to come.

Looking from his vantage point into the distant future, Daniel wrote that "there shall be a time of trouble, such as never was since there was a nation, even to that time" (Daniel 12:1). An interesting phrase: "Such as never was." If we're reading that correctly, Daniel is talking about something worse than Auschwitz, worse than the killing fields of Cambodia, and worse than Rwanda.

I hasten to add that I find myself talking much more about the coming Christ than I do about the coming crisis. But we can't deny what the Bible has to say. The mother of all crises is still yet to come.

And what I've learned over the years is that many people will consider those words and shudder in their boots. The idea of a time of trouble, a period of tribulation, fills many people with dread. "How will I ever be able to face it?" they ask. "What will happen to my children?" Fair questions. But not really necessary questions.

It is evident that we can have confidence in the midst of

chaos if we are connected by faith to Jesus. He calmed the storm on the Sea of Galilee. And God delivered His people from marauding armies and bloodthirsty enemies in the most dramatic fashion on multiple occasions.

But having said that, we must not forget that James went to prison and was executed (Acts 12:2), angry mobs stoned Paul to the point where those who witnessed it thought he was dead (Acts 14:19), and Jesus Himself was nailed to a cross (Matthew 27:35; Mark 15:25; Luke 23:26; John 19:18). God's faithfulness does not always result in His followers escaping a situation unscathed, but it always demonstrates to the entire universe that He can be trusted under any circumstance.

In fact, Jesus promised His followers that they would have periods of trial. He said in John 16:33, "In the world you will have tribulation; but be of good cheer, I have overcome the world." Paul told Timothy that "all who desire to live godly in Christ Jesus will suffer persecution" (2 Timothy 3:12).

We need to keep something vital in mind. The goal in our Christian lives isn't to escape all harm and trouble, to avoid every crisis. Rather, it is to vindicate the character of God in every situation, be it a period of trial or a time of joy.

The universe is looking on to see whether God's people are willing to give honor and glory to God irrespective of the situation in which they find themselves. In that sense it is almost necessary that trials—in some form—enter the lives of those who call themselves followers of Jesus. If Christianity was simply a matter of believing in Him and no longer having any more problems, people would be followers of Christ for all the wrong reasons.[2] It is as God's people live lives of faith and trust under even the most difficult circumstances that they exonerate Him from all the charges Satan has made against His character.

The Bible leaves us in no doubt that the last days of earth's history will be ones of real crisis. The book of Revelation—given by God to shine a light on history's final moments—describes the situation for us.

Confidence in Chaos

"Then I stood on the sand of the sea. And I saw a beast rising up out of the sea, having seven heads and ten horns, and on his horns ten crowns, and on his heads a blasphemous name. Now the beast which I saw was like a leopard, his feet were like the feet of a bear, and his mouth like the mouth of a lion. The dragon gave him his power, his throne, and great authority. And I saw one of his heads as if it had been mortally wounded, and his deadly wound was healed. And all the world marveled and followed the beast. So they worshiped the dragon who gave authority to the beast; and they worshiped the beast, saying, 'Who is like the beast? Who is able to make war with him?' And he was given a mouth speaking great things and blasphemies, and he was given authority to continue for forty-two months. Then he opened his mouth in blasphemy against God, to blaspheme His name, His tabernacle, and those who dwell in heaven. It was granted to him to make war with the saints and to overcome them. And authority was given him over every tribe, tongue, and nation. All who dwell on the earth will worship him, whose names have not been written in the Book of Life of the Lamb slain from the foundation of the world" (Revelation 13:1-8).

The beast John saw is a nation[3] that will have so much influence over the world before Jesus returns that John could write that the whole earth "will worship him" (verse 8). In response to the authority exerted by the first beast of Revelation 13, God calls everyone in the world to "worship Him who made heaven and earth, the sea and springs of water" (Revelation 14:7).

Acting under the leadership of Satan (the dragon of Revelation 13:2), this blasphemous power persecutes God's people. Not only will those who do not accept its dominion be unable to buy and sell (verse 17), those who do not yield their lives to it will find themselves sentenced to die (verse 15).

So we see that earth's final crisis will come about as a

certain agency seeks to receive the worship of the world, threatening with death those who refuse to engage in its un-biblical worship. The final crisis—one the world has yet to experience—is of a religious nature and will center on the subject of worship.

And in order to understand the impending last-days crisis better, we can simply look back in time and consider the experience of Daniel, Shadrach, Meshach, and Abednego. Those four men passed through times of similar trial, and their stories help us understand not only the crisis ahead, but how we may have confidence in the midst of it.

Daniel and his friends were no strangers to traumatic situations. The book of Daniel opens with their hometown, Jerusalem, under attack from the kingdom of Babylon. Led by King Nebuchadnezzar, Babylon's armies sacked Jerusalem and took away—along with enormous wealth—the flower of the Jewish youth. Nebuchadnezzar was wise enough and heartless enough to realize the benefit of educating Israel's brightest young minds to advance his own interests.

After arriving in Babylon, Daniel faced his first, but certainly not his last, crisis. As part of the training program for some of the captives of Israel to serve in Babylon, Nebuchadnezzar intended to feed the young men from his own kitchen and provide for them wine from his own cellar. But Daniel's commitment to God would not permit him to "defile himself with the portion of the king's delicacies, nor with the wine which he drank; therefore he requested of the chief of the eunuchs that he might not defile himself" (Daniel 1:8).

Daniel not only ran the risk of being a pain in the royal neck, but of greatly offending a king who had already shown he was more than willing to shed Jewish blood. Telling the king "thanks, but no thanks" wasn't likely to do much for either Daniel's future career prospects or for his present well-being. So he proposed that he and his three friends be allowed a vegetarian diet for 10 days, at the end of which their captors would monitor the young men's health. The Bible says that as a result, Daniel and company were far in advance of those who ate from the Babylonian royal menu.

Thus Daniel learned early in Babylon that faithfulness to God would result in divine blessing. It would also lead him into precarious situations that would place his life in jeopardy, but he knew from experience that he could trust God even in a crisis. *Especially* in a crisis.

In Daniel 2 King Nebuchadnezzar has—and then promptly forgets—a remarkable dream. Unable to tell the king what he had dreamed and what it meant, the royal counselors found themselves sentenced to death. And as Daniel, Shadrach, Meshach and Abednego now belonged among the king's advisors, the royal decree applied to them. "The decree went out, and they began killing the wise men; and they sought Daniel and his companions, to kill them" (Daniel 2:13).

Now, *that's* a crisis in anybody's language! Daniel and his friends faced death for something they had no part in and no control over. When he understood the reason for the executions, "Daniel went in and asked the king to give him time, that he might tell the king the interpretation" (verse 16). Gathering his friends together with him, the group of four young men prayed that God would give them wisdom regarding the king's dream and spare their lives.

God answered their prayer in a spectacular way, and Daniel was able to explain the dream to the king. He told Nebuchadnezzar that the king had dreamed of an image (or idol) constructed largely from four different metals. As we saw in a previous chapter, it had a head made of gold, a chest and arms of silver, a midsection of bronze, legs of iron, and feet of a mixture of iron and clay (verses 31-36). A rock (representing Jesus) smashed into it (at the time of Jesus' second coming) and destroyed the image.

The four metals represented four kingdoms that would

rule during successive eras in the world's history. And Nebuchadnezzar learned that the head of the image—the head of gold—represented his kingdom, Babylon.

In a certain sense, Nebuchadnezzar should have felt great pride in hearing Daniel announce that he was—that his kingdom was—the head of gold. But Daniel had bad news for the mighty king. The kingdom represented by the chest and arms of silver would succeed—and therefore likely conquer—that of Babylon.

While Nebuchadnezzar appreciated Daniel's wisdom—making him "ruler over the whole province of Babylon" and appointing Shadrach, Meshach and Abednego to be "over the affairs of the province of Babylon" (verses 48, 49)—he never did forget that God's message to him was that his kingdom would one day pass away.

Evidently that thought became more than the proud monarch could bear. In Daniel 3 the king had his artisans construct an enormous idol made of gold in defiance of the Word of God. He would not be merely the head of gold—the entire image would consist of it! The king of Babylon intended that, contrary to the Word of God, his kingdom would have no end. "Is not this great Babylon, that I have built . . . ?" he asked in Daniel 4:30. An inscription made by Nebuchadnezzar and discovered in the ruins of ancient Babylon reads, "Thus I completely made strong the defences of Babylon. May it last forever!"[4]

Erecting the golden image in a prominent location, Nebuchadnezzar called people from all over his kingdom to the dedication of the great statue. And when the people had assembled before the king's golden idol, he commanded everyone to "fall down and worship the gold image that King Nebuchadnezzar has set up" (Daniel 3:5).

For an ordinary Babylonian, such a command posed no problem at all, especially if the king himself ordered it. Worshipping an idol was consistent with the social, cultural, and religious mores of the day. Nobody in the crowd would have given the king's orders a second thought. Except for Shadrach, Meshach, and Abednego.

The Bible does not reveal the reason Daniel was not present on the day Nebuchadnezzar inaugurated the idol, but his three friends were in the vast crowd on the plain of Dura, and when the king ordered the masses to bow, they knew it was not business as usual.

The king had said, "Whoever does not fall down and worship shall be cast immediately into the midst of a burning fiery furnace" (verse 6). What would the three young men do? What *could* they do? They each faced a choice between loyalty to God and the sentence of death, or disloyalty to God and life. And because they refused to bow to the image at the appointed time, the king sentenced them to die in the furnace (verse 15).

The crisis faced by Shadrach, Meshach, and Abednego presages the one during earth's final days. A powerful authority erected an image and commanded worship contrary to the Word of God. God's people faced a great decision—obedience or disobedience. And the consequence would be either life or death.

A similar scenario plays out in Daniel 6, which, like Daniel 3, foreshadows the great crisis of the earth's final days.

Following the defeat of Babylon by the kingdom of Medo-Persia, the political leaders of the latter were so envious of Daniel's elevation to a position of authority that they plotted to end his life. Knowing that he was unfailingly faithful to God, they sought to catch him in a trap based on worship.

They proposed to the king "that whoever petitions any god or man for thirty days, except you, O king, shall be cast into the den of lions" (Daniel 6:7). For Daniel to pray to the king rather than to the God of heaven was unthinkable, which meant that he would certainly sentence himself to death. How he reacted in this time of crisis demonstrated not only remarkable faith but faith in a remarkable God.

"Now when Daniel knew that the writing was signed, he went home. And in his upper room, with his windows open toward Jerusalem, he knelt down on his knees three times that day, and prayed and gave thanks before his God, as was his custom since early days" (verse 10).

Fully aware that choosing the true worship of the God of heaven would lead to a death sentence, Daniel defied the decree of the king. He prayed at home, where others could easily observe him. Not only that, he prayed with his windows open, not attempting to hide what he was doing.[5] And he didn't pray just once—for which the king might have been able to choose lenience—but three times, and he prayed on his knees so that anyone spying on him would have no doubt as to what Daniel was doing. Further, he prayed facing toward Jerusalem. Nobody would think he was complying with the decree by praying in the direction of the royal palace. As with the experience of his friends in chapter 3, Daniel faced a law mandating false worship, with the death penalty levied against anyone violating it.

The book of Daniel, the companion to the book of Revelation, outlines for us in these two stories the conflict looming over the world. The scenario portrayed in Revelation is of a world-ruling power—interestingly, referred to as "Babylon" in Revelation 17 and 18—enforcing laws that mandate worship contrary to the law of God. And the penalties for refusing to bow down to the image will once again be severe.

We see in Revelation 13 that the issue will be global. "All the world" (Revelation 13:3; cf. verse 8) follows the beast of Bible prophecy, and the world will pass through a time of terrible tribulation (see Matthew 24:21).

How should people of faith react to the scenes about to unfold before them? Perhaps it would be wise to consider how those caught in the midst of the issues in the book of Daniel responded to them.

The Bible records that Shadrach, Meshach, and Abednego

were resolute in their faith in God. "O Nebuchadnezzar, we have no need to answer you in this matter. If that is the case, our God whom we serve is able to deliver us from the burning fiery furnace, and He will deliver us from your hand, O king. But if not, let it be known to you, O king, that we do not serve your gods, nor will we worship the gold image which you have set up" (Daniel 3:16-18).

They had decided ahead of time that they would be faithful to God. And they believed that if it was His will to do so, God was able to deliver them from death in the furnace. But they made it clear to Nebuchadnezzar that if they could only purchase their lives through compromising their allegiance to God, they would sooner die than live.

Uppermost in their minds was His honor. They would perish rather than deny Him, and they knew that if they were faithful to God, it would give Him the opportunity to show Himself to be who He truly is.

Having cast the three young men into the fiery furnace, King Nebuchadnezzar was astonished to see "four men loose, walking in the midst of the fire; and they are not hurt, and the form of the fourth is like the Son of God" (verse 25).

God delivered Shadrach, Meshach, and Abednego in a dramatic way. With the furnace heated seven times hotter than usual—so hot that the men who hurled them into the furnace themselves perished from its heat—Shadrach, Meshach, and Abednego were not so much as singed by the flames. And as they stood for God in the midst of that fire, One "like the Son of God" stood beside them.

When they came forth from the fiery furnace, the pagan king Nebuchadnezzar was so affected by what he had witnessed that he spoke passionately in praise of the God of heaven. Later he became a believer in the God of heaven (see Daniel 4:37), something that might never have happened if the three men had not been faithful in their walk with God. How many others the incident impressed that day we do not know, but from that day to this, countless millions have heard the story of God's great deliverance and the confidence of His followers in the midst of a crisis.

In Daniel 6 royal guards cast Daniel into a den of lions as punishment for breaking the law of the Medo-Persian king. Realizing that his advisors had essentially duped him into signing a law that would condemn Daniel to death, the king was filled with regret for what he had done. That night he couldn't sleep and did not eat. He went to the lions' den the next morning and called, saying, "Daniel, servant of the living God, has your God, whom you serve continually, been able to deliver you from the lions?" (Daniel 6:20).

"My God sent His angel and shut the lions' mouths," Daniel replied, "so that they have not hurt me, because I was found innocent before Him; and also, O king, I have done no wrong before you" (verse 22). And as in the case of his three friends, Daniel's faithfulness had a huge impact on the king.

King Darius, the Medo-Persia king, issued an edict: "I make a decree that in every dominion of my kingdom men must tremble and fear before the God of Daniel. For He is the living God, and steadfast forever; His kingdom is the one which shall not be destroyed, and His dominion shall endure to the end. He delivers and rescues, and He works signs and wonders in heaven and on earth, who has delivered Daniel from the power of the lions" (verses 26, 27).

Looking ahead to the crisis of earth's final days, we can have confidence in God's faithfulness and power. Should He choose to do so, He is able to deliver His people from crisis. But should He not decide to do so, He is able to sustain them in the midst of crisis.

God has not rescued many heroes of faith from the bitterest of crises. The authorities relentlessly and brutally persecuted the early Christian church. The Anabaptists of sixteenth- and seventeenth-century Europe; the Huguenots of France in the seventeenth and eighteenth centuries; the Moravians of Bohemia in the eighteenth century—all of these groups suffered intense persecution, and while God delivered some from the crises they faced, He sustained others to endure the hardships that came to them.

God rescued Peter, the impetuous disciple of Jesus, from prison and certain death, but not James. Martin Luther did not die a martyr's death, while Huss, Jerome, Cranmer, Ridley, Latimer and so many other great men and women of faith did.[6]

But in each case the believer in Jesus had *confidence in the midst of a crisis*, and honored God by their example and faith.

The Lord has repeatedly and consistently demonstrated that He is faithful and good. Anyone who believes that—based on an experience in God's Word and a personal knowledge of Him—will be sustained through any difficulty. It does not mean that life will be devoid of trials, but that God is able to keep us even in difficult times.

The question for you and me to answer doesn't concern how we'll fare when future trials come, nor does it matter whether or not crises will ever confront us. The questions for a believer in Jesus to answer are simply "Do I know God, and can I trust Him? Am I in a saving relationship with Jesus Christ?"

Salvation is not just for "good" people, and it isn't only for "other" people. Jesus died so that you might know Him and have a confidence in God in this world that will see you one day walk on streets of gold in heaven. Between now and then you can face the world with confidence—confidence that you are forgiven of your sins, confidence that God has accepted you, and confidence that when Jesus returns He will take you to be with Him. Forever.

In 2013 CNN reported on the remarkable story of a young man in India and his touching relationship with his mother. In 1993 Vijaya Kumari went to prison for a crime in which she denied any involvement. The court granted bail, which it set at 5,000 Indian rupees, which in 2013 converted to about US$89. But nobody from her family came forward to help Vijaya, and she remained in prison.

Pregnant when she entered prison, Vijaya gave birth four months later to a son. At 6 years of age Vijaya's son went to live in a remand home for children until his release at the age of 13. The son, Kanhaiya, determined as a child that when he was old enough he would work to raise the money needed to secure his mother's release. Nineteen years after first imprisoned, Vijaya Kumari walked free, thanks to a loving son who did all he could to buy her freedom.

Two thousand years ago Jesus Christ died on a cross at a place called Calvary, just outside the walls of the city of Jerusalem. He did that to pay the price of your sins, and when He died your debt was paid. You can now walk free—free from sin and guilt, and free to live the "abundant life" (see John 10:10) Jesus came to give you.

What will you do with what Jesus has done for you? You could ignore it and go on with your life independent of God, or you could accept it and receive Him into your life.

If you have already accepted Jesus, you can recommit your life to Him, secure in His goodness and assured of His faithfulness.

One day Jesus is going to return to earth. Between now and then there will be that "time of trouble" Daniel wrote of in Daniel 12:1. I wouldn't recommend that you keep your eyes trained on the coming crisis. When you're driving in a storm, you focus on the road, not on the storm clouds. If you can see the way home, there's every likelihood you'll arrive there safely. But if you look at the storm it is more likely you'll meet with tragedy.

Jesus is our "way" home. He said in John 14:6, "I am the way, the truth, and the life. No one comes to the Father except through Me." Or: "Through Me you can come to the Father" and to everlasting life.

John wrote in 1 John 5:12 that "he who has the Son has life," and in the very next verse said, "These things I have written to you who believe in the name of the Son of God, that you may know that you have eternal life, and that you may continue to believe in the name of the Son of God" (verse 13).

"I've told you these things *so that you may know* that you have eternal life." And if you know you have eternal life, you'll have confidence in the midst of chaos.

------

[1] "Selection" divided people into two groups: those who would work at the camp, and those sent for immediate extermination.

[2] See the story in John 6:22-29. Jesus had huge crowds of people following Him because they believed Jesus was about to expel the hated Romans and return Israel to power and prosperity. When He told them His being on the earth was so they could learn to eat His flesh and drink His blood—to accept Him as Savior in all His humility—their interest rapidly diminished, and they "walked with Him no more."

[3] Bible prophecy uses the imagery of a beast as a symbol for a kingdom or nation. See Daniel 7:17-19, 23.

[4] George Rawlinson, *The Seven Great Monarchies of the Ancient Eastern World* (New York: John B. Alden, 1885), Vol. II, p. 261.

[5] I would have understood if Daniel had prayed in a locked closet in order to avoid detection.

[6] Many died for Jesus while singing His praises.

NOTES

NOTES

NOTES

NOTES

NOTES

They Didn't Believe in Jesus.
He Showed Up Anyway.

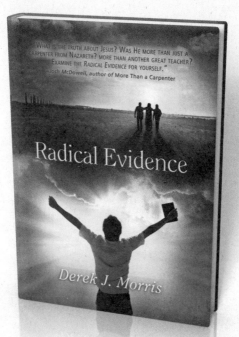

An angry young atheist. A Muslim. An African ancestor worshipper. *Radical Evidence* introduces you to people who've had a dramatic encounter with the Messiah they didn't believe in. Author Derek Morris also includes amazing prophecies from the Bible that pointed forward to events in the life of Christ. If you have questions, or you have a friend or family member who struggles with doubts, this book presents some surprising evidence for a real Jesus. Hardcover, 128 pages. 978-0-8127-0514-0. **DVD:** Four presentations, approx. 28 minutes each. 978-1-936929-07-8.

A World of Resources

There is More Online

Looking for more Bible studies? Discover It Is Written's online Bible school. FREE courses include:

- Unsealing Daniel's Mysteries
- New Beginnings
- Search for Certainty

Find a world of spiritual resources at:

www.itiswritten.com

IT IS WRITTEN

Free Bible Guides

A dynamic way to become better acquainted with your Bible.

The DISCOVER BIBLE GUIDES are designed for busy people like you. They will help bring your Bible to life and you can study at home at your own pace. There is no cost or obligation. The DISCOVER BIBLE GUIDES are available online or you can request them by writing to It Is Written, Box O, Thousand Oaks, CA 91359. Or call now and begin a new adventure with your Bible.

CALL TODAY
1-800-253-3000
OR LOG ONTO
www.itiswritten.com

IT IS WRITTEN